D1501472

HIS
ADVENT
Still His Greatest Gift

Rebekah J. Freelan

WestBow
PRESS

WestBow Press books may be ordered through booksellers or by contacting:

WestBow Press
A Division of Thomas Nelson
1663 Liberty Drive
Bloomington, IN 47403
www.westbowpress.com
1-(866) 928-1240

Because of the dynamic nature of the Internet, any Web addresses or links contained in
this book may have changed since publication and may no longer be valid. The views
expressed in this work are solely those of the author and do not necessarily reflect the
views of the publisher, and the publisher hereby disclaims any responsibility for them.

ISBN: 978-1-4497-0181-9 (sc)
ISBN: 978-1-4497-0182-6 (e)

Library of Congress Control Number: 2010926335

Printed in the United States of America

WestBow Press rev. date: 6/11/2010

Dedication

To my parents, Dave and Marilyn Freelan. You taught me to know and love the Bible, and you sacrificed so I could write. For both things...and much more...I'm grateful.

Introduction

What is Advent? I asked myself that question one particularly sluggish Christmas season.

I know it is the Christian approach to Christmas. I know every Sunday in church, we light a candle...sometimes purple, sometimes pink, sometimes white...always accompanied by a reading. I know Advent is observed by some as a countdown to Christmas Day...complete with pieces of chocolate hidden in cardboard calendars.

But what is it really? Is Advent just chocolate and candles? Or is there more? Is there something about Advent that can help my heart find Christmas?

That year I learned Advent is about an *arrival*. About His presence. Throughout the month, I studied the Scriptures and found new meaning in the moments when a Man who changed everything arrived in the lives of people who lived 2000 years ago. For the first time, I saw these people not as halo-encircled beings in the nativity lineup or characters in a dramatic production of "life in that day," but as real people. The hurt and lonely, the anxious and hopeful, the confused and afraid, the ignorant and ostracized. Each of them met the Savior of the world and as He arrived and became tangible in their lives, He left them forever changed. His arrival brought a gift of hope to those who needed it...and accepted it.

As I read...as I studied...I saw myself in each of those people. Though I may not have lived in circumstances identical to any of them, I understood the feelings of their hearts. The fear, the frustration, the faith. And as I saw how the Master moved in and through their lives, I better understood how He moves through my own. I began to understand more about the moments when His presence came near even though I wasn't purposefully seeking after Him.

And finally, it made sense. For thousands of years, the world had awaited the Advent of a Savior. The arrival of a new Hope. And just as God promised, Jesus arrived to fulfill that longing. And amid my annual traditions, He awaits the invitation of Advent in my heart. He longs to meet my need, yes...meet my desires, yes...but most of all...to meet <u>me</u>.

Christmas is busier than any other time of year. But I invite you to take a few moments each day to sit with me and peek into the past. To see these people who knew Jesus in the flesh. To learn from their encounters. And most of all, to welcome His arrival in a fresh way and invite His presence to remain with you this season and in all days.

Author's Note

The Word of God is a Treasure that deserves to be greatly respected and carefully interpreted. 2 Timothy 2:15 says "Do your best to present yourself to God as one approved, a workman who does not need to be ashamed and who correctly handles the word of truth."

My goal *always*, when studying Scripture, is to handle with care the words that are Divinely inspired. In my writing of this Advent study, I've tried to imagine the thoughts and feelings of the people who met the Savior. After all, they were real people who experienced emotions never recorded...perhaps anywhere. But I've also tried to follow very closely the facts that Scripture declares. In order to distinguish the information that is specifically pulled from the Bible, you will find endnotes throughout the reading that will direct you to the Scripture references which contain that information.

As for the rest, please read in the spirit I wrote...

December 1

But Mary treasured up all these things and pondered them in her heart.
Luke 2:19

When did Mary first encounter her Son, her Savior?

Did she know the minute the Holy Spirit engulfed her and she conceived the Messiah?[1]

If she did, she may have felt a warm rush embrace her and known in that instant that the Son of God had begun to grow beneath her heart.

And as He grew there safely hidden in the secret place, as God His Father created His inmost being…knit Him together in His mother's womb…as all the days ordained for Him were written in God's great book before one of them came to be[2]…did He grow within her heart even as He grew beneath it?

Did Mary consider her first meeting with Him that mysterious day when He rustled within her for the first time? That day women speak of and yet none understand so well until they feel the soft tickling of butterfly movement?

Or was it the moment when she brought forth her firstborn Son and laid him in a manger because there was no room for them in the inn?[3] The moment her eyes linked with His for the first time? The moment His skin touched hers? The moment His cry reached her ears?

When did she meet Him?

We will never know for sure.

But that moment…that one fragment of time in the stable…never left her mind. She saw it, savored it, longed for it, as she stood at the foot of her Son's cross,[4] watching Him gasp for His final breaths just as she had watch Him gasp for His first.

Mary is the only one we know for sure was there as Jesus slid from eternity into humanity and back again. We might speculate that the innkeeper's kind wife or Joseph himself stayed by her side as she labored and delivered, but we don't know. Scripture only says "she gave birth to her firstborn, a son. She wrapped him in cloths and placed him in a manger, because there was no room for them in the inn."[5]

We've all heard ideas of how it might have been. How tired she was after trekking to Bethlehem in her third trimester. How late at night when

1

they arrived at the inn. How rude the innkeeper as he turned them away. How scared she was to endure her first childbirth away from everyone she knew. How shunned she had been since news of her scandalous pregnancy broke. How worried and helpless Joseph felt as he watched her suffer. But we don't really know if it happened that way at all.

Whether or not she had a long and painful labor, whether or not she was scared and alone, surely she was overwhelmed. Mothers cry at the first glimpse of their newborn children. Cry with relief that the labor has ended. Cry with joy at the arrival they've awaited so long. Cry with wonder at the perfection of their tiny offspring. Cry with the incredible realization of responsibility before them.

And just as Jesus' fragile, infant life depended upon Mary, Mary's fragile, sinful soul depended upon Jesus. Imagine that realization settling upon Mary as she wrapped Him in cloths and placed Him in a manger. She began her role of motherhood doing what mothers do…making a way to care for their children, through whatever resourceful methods they find.

Did Mary understand *Jesus*? Did she understand as she met Him, examined Him, learned Him as mothers do…that He was *Jesus*?

Perhaps she did in the most naïve way. The angel had simply said to Mary, "Greetings, you who are highly favored! The Lord is with you… Do not be afraid, Mary, you have found favor with God. You will be with child and give birth to a son, and you are to give him the name Jesus. He will be great and will be called the Son of the Most High. The Lord God will give him the throne of his father David, and he will reign over the house of Jacob forever; his kingdom will never end…The Holy Spirit will come upon you, and the power of the Most High will overshadow you. So the holy one to be born will be called the Son of God…For nothing is impossible with God."[6]

The most basic instruction. It was all she knew. Her greeting to her cousin Elizabeth[7] shows that she understood God's intention to keep His promise to His people through this Baby, so she understood enough of Jewish law to know that. But Mary didn't need to *know* Jewish law to raise the Son of God. He could learn the law in the Temple. Mary simply needed *God*. She found favor with Him…He chose her…and He stayed with her, enabling her to do each task as it came to be.

Would God ask a young mother at the manger-side of her newborn Son to look ahead to His execution? We don't know. But she knew this

Son of hers was extraordinary and the journey to raise Him would have to be Spirit-led. She wasn't to fear. The angel had said so.

Mary probably didn't look to the cross that day. The day of Jesus' birth was a day for her to count fingers and toes, caress soft skin, brush kisses across a brow, and simply hold the warm, wriggling Baby. To smile at His big yawns, comfort His whimpering newborn cries, and feel His breath blow warmly across her hand while she felt to see if He did still breathe.

A woman of such few words. Perhaps this is how she came to be chosen as the honored mother of the Messiah. When the angel appeared to announce God's life-plan for her, she asked one question – *How will this be, since I am a virgin?*[8] – and offered one answer – *I am the Lord's servant. May it be to me as you have said.*[9]

Mary was not a typical woman. Most would have badgered the angel with a list of inquisitions. Most would have exclaimed no less than two dozen times that this could not be real. Most would have offered excuses and expressed doubts.

Mary asked and accepted. The next words we hear from her, she uttered at the side of Elizabeth:

> *My soul glorifies the Lord and my spirit rejoices in God my Savior,*
> *for he has been mindful of the humble state of his servant.*
> *From now on all generations will call me blessed,*
> *for the Mighty One has done great things for me – holy is his name.*[10]

Mary recognized God's blessing upon her. She acknowledged His might, His mercy, His justice, His help, and His faithfulness. And then she fell silent.

From the very start…from conception to childbirth to childhood to crucifixion…she saw how special Jesus was and she kept their bond sacred and secret. The moment she met Jesus was wealth unlike any other. She cherished that precious knowledge so deeply within her heart that perhaps even Joseph never knew. They were hers alone.

The Message says, *Mary kept all these things to herself, holding them dear, deep within herself.*[11]

Jesus' arrival, whether the first time or the fifteen hundredth time, can be a deeply private experience. One so sacred perhaps it cannot be adequately put into words. One so personal that to share it would be a betrayal of intimacy.

December 2

And he gave him the name Jesus.
Matthew 1:25b

Joseph was one of very few…perhaps even just two…who met Jesus before He was *Jesus.*

Scripture is silent about the details of this birth. Was Joseph at Mary's side as she gave birth? Was he out scouring the unfamiliar neighborhood for someone…anyone…who could help his precious wife bring a baby into the world? Did he return to the stable with a helper in tow only to find the Baby already born and resting inside the cloths Mary used to wrap Him?[1] Did he pace nervously outside the door of the stable, straining to hear that first cry?

Wherever Joseph was the moment the Baby entered the world, his own world forever changed. It had begun to change nine months earlier during what was perhaps a restless night of sleep. Somehow he'd received the news that his darling Mary was expecting a baby. One he knew was not his own.[2] And as he wrestled with the loss of his love and the preservation of his integrity and family name,[3] "an angel of the Lord appeared to him in a dream and said, 'Joseph, son of David, do not be afraid to take Mary home as your wife, because what is conceived in her is from the Holy Spirit. She will give birth to a son, and you are to give him the name Jesus, because he will save his people from their sins.'"[4]

You are to give him the name Jesus. Joseph's role as Jesus' earthly father began with that assignment. God wanted him to name the Baby.

To think about the adjustments Joseph had to make in his life-plan shows that to the very core, he was a man of character and integrity. We credit Mary with being a gentle, loving young woman who earned the role of Jesus' mother because of her dedication to the Lord. But Joseph had to bear the same qualities. How else would he have been fit to be the example to Jesus that bore witness to the Heavenly Father?

Joseph trusted God. This we know because, "When Joseph woke up, he did what the angel of the Lord had commanded him and took Mary home as his wife."[5] He didn't seek a medium to interpret his dream. He didn't blame the bizarre happening on a surplus of spicy cuisine. He trusted the Voice he heard because he knew the Lord.

Joseph showed restraint. The Message says, "But he did not consummate the marriage until she had the baby."[6] He lived under the same roof with the woman he had grown to love – and yet for nine months he put aside his own needs and desires so the prophecy would be fulfilled – "The *virgin* will be with child and will give birth to a son, and they will call him Immanuel – which means, 'God with us.'"[7]

Joseph respected Mary. Before the angel's visit, when he weighed his options, he "did not want to expose her to public disgrace, so he had in mind to divorce her quietly."[8] He truly cared about how the enormity of his decision would impact her. And though he may have had every reason to humiliate her before everyone they knew, that was not in keeping with his character.

Joseph obeyed. When the Child was born, he could have chosen to tell well-meaning baby-gawkers in the marketplace that Jesus was his own flesh and blood. He could have ignored God's command and given Him an expected family name. Or a name he and Mary had picked out during a secret romantic walk as they courted and dreamed of their future. But Joseph gave him the name *Jesus*. The name chosen by God Himself.[9]

What did Joseph think as he crouched beside the makeshift crib and absorbed the sight of a new Life? Did he have a twinge of resentment for this Baby Who had come rather obtrusively into his life? Did he wring his hands with worry over how he would provide for three instead of two? Did he cast a furtive glance toward the door watching for intruders who might disrupt the exhausted mother and Child? Did he implore Heaven for wisdom in how to raise the Son of God to be a man?

Or did he only dream of days to come? Did he envision a Toddler hesitantly taking tiny steps in sawdust? Did he make a mental note to craft a tiny tool set out of wood for Jesus to play with while He visited the carpenter shop?[10] Did he imagine a day when this Boy would enter the temple and begin to learn even as he may have once done in his own boyhood?

Did Joseph have any idea what this Boy would mean? As he stood over the manger and uttered Jesus' name to Him for the first time, did he know what that name would cost the family? The midnight escape from Herod's bloody massacre?[11] The panic when He came up missing on a family journey?[12] The lump in his own throat when Jesus declared to everyone that He must be about His Father's business, and Joseph was not the father He meant?[13] Mary's tears and heartbreak as she stood beneath the cross of her strong and gentle Son and found herself entrusted to the care of His best friend?[14]

Had he known, would he have uttered the Name? He had no choice. Amid joy or heartbreak, this Baby was God's chosen path of salvation for the world.[15] This was not his own Son. This was God's *only* Son. His own sons would someday come into the world. His time to create flesh and bone with Mary was yet to be.[16] For now, his responsibility was to declare this Baby to be Jesus.

Joseph is so scarcely mentioned in the Bible. His role as Jesus' father was overshadowed by Jesus' true Father. The firstborn of the family was the Firstborn of Creation[17] and to focus on Joseph might lead us to forget Jesus' Father. But somehow Joseph knew his role and accepted the shadows, even embraced them.

The moment the Baby arrived, he declared this Baby was Jesus.

He declared simultaneously to his Father and Son that this was Immanuel.

And in that moment of meeting, Joseph accepted a life of uncertainty. A life he had not envisioned. A path he couldn't possibly have prepared for. And yet he accepted a role no other father has ever known – a gift so great perhaps he could not even fully grasp it himself.

When Jesus arrives, He brings a life we cannot envision. A life perhaps very different from the one we have imagined for ourselves.

To declare His name is to give up our own claim and to instead accept His claim over us.

To become His means we step into the shadows and allow the light of the true Father to shine brightly.

Yet to give him the name Jesus is to accept that He is with us. That He has saved us from our sins. That new life has begun because His new Life began.

December 3

So they hurried off and found Mary and Joseph, and the baby, who was lying in the manger. When they had seen him, they spread the word concerning what had been told them about this child, and all who heard it were amazed at what the shepherds said to them.
Luke 2:16-18

The Shepherd of our souls selected a group of shepherds to receive Jesus' spectacular birth announcement.

The night was probably an ordinary one for them. They might have gathered about in the field, swapping stories they'd heard before but loved to tell again and again. Perhaps one was about the birth of a lamb.

Little did they know that not too far away, a Lamb had just been born.[1]

A rustling…a sound. Experience would have brought them instantly to their feet, weapons drawn, ready to fend off the intruder and protect the lambs in their care.

But it wasn't an animal. No lion or bear lumbered toward them. In fact, what was it? The shepherds trembled in a blaze of glorious light as the angel of the Lord moved closer.[2]

> *Do not be afraid.*
> *I bring you good news of great joy that will be for all the people.*
> *Today in the town of David a Savior has been born to you;*
> *he is Christ the Lord.*
> *This will be a sign to you:*
> *You will find the baby wrapped in cloths and lying in a manger.*[3]

What went through their minds as they stood…or perhaps crouched, still trembling…before the angel? Did they wonder if they were collectively hallucinating? Was this a practical joke from a fellow team of shepherds?

Before they could even shake their heads or swallow the lumps that seemed lodged in their throats, "a great company of the heavenly host appeared with the angel, praising God and saying, 'Glory to God in the highest, and on earth peace to men on whom his favor rests.'"[4]

The angel choir evaporated into the heavens in just moments,[5] and the shepherds were left to stare at one another in dazed wonder.

Why them? Why a bunch of confirmed bachelors in desperate need of bathing and newer clothes? People usually went to great lengths to keep their babies away from the smelly, manner-challenged lot of animal watchers. Had any of them even been near a newborn before? Had any of them seen the wonder of an infant chest rising and falling with first breaths? Aside from their wooly charges, had they seen such a tiny life?

They were considered by some, surely, to be the least of the community. And yet that is exactly who this Baby had come to serve.[6] Why should He wait until His ministry began to meet those whose lives He came to save? Why should their names not be the first in the list of visitors inscribed in His baby book? He had come, after all, to make a way for their names to be inscribed in another Book…the Lamb's Book of Life.[7]

Why *not* shepherds? In fact, who *but* them?

The forgotten and lowly were the sought and chosen ones. Under the dark cover of night, when the rest of the community lay tucked beneath blankets on their floor pallets, God the Father lit up the night sky for the faithful few still on duty.

And not only did He announce the birth of His Son, but He invited them to go and find Jesus. He sent them on a scavenger hunt of the city – leading them to the type of place they knew best – a barn.[8] He told these shepherds the Baby had come for *them*. He would be in a manger.[9] Shepherds knew about mangers.

Scripture indicates they wasted very little time. As the last of the angels ascended from where they came, the shepherds didn't even hesitate, but set out for the tiny town. Set out in search of a Savior. [10]

We don't know how long it took them to find the right barn. Perhaps by the time they trekked into Bethlehem and through the streets, morning had come. Maybe it was still late at night, but being shepherds, they didn't stop to think about the protocol of waiting until daybreak to knock on the door. After all…they were up. Why shouldn't a new family be awake also?

Nothing is recorded about their meeting. They may have burst into the stable with heavy footsteps and bumbling gestures, startling the poor family inside. Maybe they peeked in a window and scrambled over each other for the first glimpse. They might have asked to see the new Baby – maybe even to hold Him.

Did Mary and Joseph rush to protect the Infant as the shepherds came tumbling into the barn, all talking at once, explaining how they knew about this birth? Did they listen, slightly amused, as the men argued with one another about various details, each insisting that it really happened *this* way?

Mary might have swallowed hard as she passed the brand new Child into the unsure arms of the first shepherd. Perhaps it was his first time to hold a baby. And in that moment, he held the Baby of all babies. They surely missed the new mother putting a trembling hand over her mouth as the shepherds carefully passed her Son from one set of arms to the next – each uncertain – but each so gentle.

And the hands of the people cradled the Savior. The One Who would later cradle their sins on His back as He indeed saved them.[11]

The shepherds had hurried to meet Him – leaving behind responsibility and expectation. And after they did meet Him, they remembered the angel had given them an assignment. This Baby was for all people.[12]

They did not keep their midnight episode a secret. Scripture says they "returned, glorifying and praising God for all the things they had heard and seen, which were just as they had been told."[13]

The original praise team.

A group of uncouth, dirty shepherds told anyone and everyone about a night when angels visited them, and they saw a new Baby asleep in a barn. And not just any Baby. A Savior.

Maybe they hadn't spent time learning much in the Jewish temple. Perhaps they didn't know the ancient prophecies. In fact, this may have been entirely new information for them. But they didn't care about what they knew and what they didn't know. They only cared about what they saw.

Meeting that Baby changed them forever.

They knew they were seen by a Father above.

They knew they were chosen to receive the news.

They knew they had beheld – and perhaps even held – their Savior.

And they could not keep it quiet.

Jesus had arrived.

And that led them to glorify and praise Him.

December 4

On coming to the house, they saw the child with his mother Mary, and they bowed down and worshiped him.
Matthew 2:11

Unlike the shepherds who may have burst rather boisterously into the stable where Jesus spent His first hours, the Magi who traveled from a great distance came about their visit in a bit more organized manner.[1]

If we put aside for just a moment all the controversy of the where and the when and the how-long-after that seems to constantly shroud these astrologers of old, we can learn from their encounter with the child Jesus.

These men – however many comprised the company – studied the heavens, the stars, and the planets.[2] And we know that sometime after Jesus' birth, they found in their routine observations, a star that looked out of sorts compared to what they regularly saw.[3] Through that finding, they began mapping out a journey – no small feat in their day. They manually calculated times and distances and charted a course while packing and planning for this trip that in their minds bore significant magnitude.[4]

Tradition leads us to envision the camel caravan that brought these wealthy travelers to Jesus' home. But regardless of their mode of transportation, they made their first destination the great city of Jerusalem, assuming, as any educated guesser would, that a king – which is what they were expecting – would live in the palace.

When King Herod heard of their quest, he pulled them aside secretly and quizzed them on the exact details of their findings.[5] Fear already rose within his heart at the thought of a covert king growing up somewhere around him.[6] He gave the Magi directions to Bethlehem and an assignment to return to him with a comprehensive route so he could pay a visit of his own.[7]

After months of observing, researching, gathering, observing some more, planning, charting, packing, and traveling, the men continued on their way, certainly with adrenaline pumping at the realization that the One they sought was so near at hand.[8] Those last few tedious miles that lay between them and Jesus must have seemed to stretch to nearly twice their length.

Perhaps as they rode, they rehearsed their speeches. After all, if they'd thoughtfully packed such lavish gifts to present, they had certainly prepared a careful speech to deliver as they bestowed the riches. Maybe they speculated how this meeting would change their lives forever. Maybe this was their big break in the world of astrology. They had worked hard to gain the position and wealth they already attained, but perhaps finding *this* King would be proof of their security in life and among all astrologers for all time.

They may have been preparing to deliver the news to royalty everywhere – starting with Herod as he had requested – and then moving their way back home, planning other stops along the way to deliver the good news.

They moved on, carefully watching the skies, their map that had brought them thus far. Scripture says, "When they saw the star, they were overjoyed."[9] The Message says it this way: "They could hardly contain themselves!"[10] Whatever the star did – whether it appeared or stopped moving or grew brighter or exploded into a million shooting stars – they knew in that moment they had arrived. The One they searched for was *there.*

As they gathered their cautiously protected gifts in their arms and moved toward the door, what entered their minds? Did nerves begin to creep in, even though they weren't sure why? Were they shocked to see such a meager house serving as the home of a King?[11] Did they wonder if they'd misread all the signs?

The Bible does not mention Joseph at all during this event. Maybe he was at work. Perhaps he was away on a trip. He might have just been down the street building a sturdy chair for an elderly woman.

When Mary came to the door to answer the call of the Magi,[12] perhaps Jesus played on the floor just a few feet away – stacking scraps of wood blocks from Joseph's carpenter shop. He may have toddled about, experimenting with the legs He'd recently discovered how to use. Maybe He crammed the rest of a snack into His mouth – trying it His own creative way now that Mary's back was turned. Or perhaps He snuggled beneath a blanket on the pallet that served as His bed – sucking His tiny thumb.

After being welcomed into the home, Scripture says "they bowed down and worshiped him."[13] All prepared speeches put aside. Gifts moved to the floor, seeming unnecessary right at that moment in time.

Just a child.

But a King.

Could the Magi have known a mere child would affect them this way? They had come to worship Him, yes, but probably a formal, obligatory sort of worship. He was a king – they were Magi. But upon entering the room, they found themselves in the presence of a *King* – One, who though barely a toddler, compelled them to bow and worship from the heart.

Ceremony could wait. Gifts could wait. Worship could not.[14]

What could Jesus do to reach the hearts of these men? Depending on His age, His vocabulary was very limited and His coordination even more so. Yet even as a toddler, He was gentle Jesus, Son of God.

How long did they worship Him? We don't know. Perhaps they knelt for several minutes, an occasional tear escaping their eyes. Maybe He even stumbled over to them, tugged at their regal garments and dried a tear with His chubby finger. Maybe His eyes lit in joy at the sight of the rich colors and textures of their clothing. He might have even begun to poke at the bags and chests that housed the great treasures intended for Him, though He could not truly appreciate them.[15]

And all the while, Mary stood in a corner, drinking in the scene of grown men with great knowledge, bowed low before her little Son who babbled and giggled at the sight of them. And while she treasured and pondered,[16] they worshiped. The Message says they were *overcome*.[17]

After they worshipped Him, they reached down and pulled out the gifts they'd selected to bring, presenting them to Jesus, even though the money and spices were hardly gifts enjoyable for a little boy.[18] Still – they knew Mary and Joseph would know and understand. Perhaps Mary's eyes grew wide as more and more treasure and wealth spilled from the bags. Her Father had seen their need! He had sent provision for His Son!

We don't know how long the Magi stayed in the presence of Jesus - perhaps just a few hours. And their journey home took a route different from the one originally planned as they avoided Herod by God's instruction.[19]

But meeting and worshiping the King surely changed more than the route home.

They arrived with a plan. They had a script, an intent, a purpose.

But Jesus' arrival drove them to their knees in worship. They bowed low, aware of His Lordship. And just His mere presence taught them that unabashed worship is far greater than planned ceremony.

December 5

Sovereign Lord, as you have promised, you now dismiss your servant in peace. For my eyes have seen your salvation, which you have prepared in the sight of all people, a light for the revelation to the Gentiles and for glory to your people Israel.
Luke 2:29-32

Simeon. An elderly man forgotten by most.[1]

Forgotten by the people in his day and forgotten by those of us who stop reading the account of Jesus' birth five verses before his part begins.[2]

Those around him probably considered him senile. They heard him talk about "the consolation of Israel."[3] What did that even mean? He walked around, smiling peacefully, insisting that he would continue to live until "the consolation of Israel" arrived.[4] People smiled politely, nodded, and scurried away before he went into full detail of whatever he meant.

To anyone who would grant him an audience, he would tell how the Holy Spirit revealed to him that he wouldn't die until the Messiah came.[5] But how long had this nation waited for the Messiah? Centuries! Did this man think he was the next Methuselah?[6]

Did Simeon himself begin to wonder if he'd heard the Holy Spirit correctly? As the telltale signs of aging settled in upon his body, did he wonder if he would really make it? The mornings when he could barely move his arthritic joints, did he sigh and begin to prepare himself for his conviction to be more of a personal dream than God's revelation to him?

As others stared at him with raised eyebrows, maybe he began to think he was all alone in his belief. Perhaps there were days when he mentioned it to no one. Days when he could not bear to see one more incredulous look from the eye of a supposed man of God.

Then came the morning.

Simeon awoke and a strange stirring rose within his soul. Something was different about this day. Could it be?

Was it possible?

"Moved by the Spirit, he went into the temple courts."[7] It may have taken every bit of effort he could muster that day to walk from wherever he lived to the Temple he loved so dearly. There was a day long before when he could easily make his way there and spend hours waiting…searching…

looking for a Holy One. That day, it took so much effort, yet a quickening in his soul pushed him to hurry...to search.

He hobbled around the courts looking, praying for God to lead him to the right place at the right time.

We don't know how it happened, but it might have gone something like this: Simeon lifted his eyes and saw a man and a young woman entering the courts.[8] The woman cradled an infant in her arms, tugging him closer to her body as they moved amid the people.

The rushing in Simeon's spirit grew stronger.

Simeon took step by painful step closer to the couple, and with each one he felt a Presence drawing near. His gaze fixed upon the bundle in the woman's arms. The Presence nestled there.

Scripture doesn't tell us what Simeon said to Mary and Joseph. We don't know if he told them the whole story from the beginning, if he stopped to inquire who they were and who this Child was, or if he simply reached out to take the Baby.

But we do know Simeon held the Son of God.[9]

This righteous man whose eyes had seen more days than most, stretched out his frail arms that now seemed renewed with strength beyond himself and accepted the Christ Child.

Perhaps his vision had blurred and dimmed with age, but today he could see clearly. He pulled back the edge of the cloths Mary had wrapped around her Son and found himself face to Face with the Savior of the world.

The Consolation of Israel napped in his arms.

Perhaps Jesus awoke and locked His baby gaze with Simeon's weathered face. What passed between God's Son and God's man in that moment? Jesus was a little over a month old.[10] He had no words to speak. And yet His very Being brought forth a burst of praise from the old man.

"Sovereign Lord, as you have promised, you now dismiss your servant in peace. For my eyes have seen your salvation..."[11]

Jesus' arrival meant that Simeon was complete.

His life as he had always known it would end.

For all he knew, he might stretch out for his afternoon nap and awaken in Glory with God the Father.

He would die. When, he didn't know. But the one thing that kept him alive had been fulfilled. His mission was accomplished. His reward granted.

Maybe, in Simeon's humanity, he wanted to hold the Child just a bit longer, to ensure another breath would pass through his own body. Maybe just seeing the Child momentarily whet his appetite to live even more – to see this Child grow in wisdom and stature…in favor with God and man.[12]

But Simeon knew the promise. He would see the Christ Child.

And he had. He held the Baby. He could go in peace.

For the Prince of Peace had arrived.

December 6

Go away from me, Lord; I am a sinful man!
Luke 5:17

The boy Jesus had grown up.

Though His official earthly ministry was in its infant stages, He had already established a reputation among the people. Even as His voice began to deepen and the whisper of a beard shadowed His pre-teen face, He had amazed the teachers and priests with His knowledge and willingness to speak out in the Temple courts.[1]

Oh yes. People knew Jesus. He was the Boy Wonder. And now the Boy was a Man – and still a wonder. People of His day probably rendered their own versions of paparazzi and celebrity stalking. Everyone wanted to be near Him and hear whatever He had to say.[2]

This particular day, He stood on a beach, no doubt taking in the beauty of a glorious sunrise, unmarred by the day which had barely awakened.[3] The only souls that stirred around Him were the fisherman who rowed closer to shore after a night of work on the water.[4]

Before the sun could even rise to its full strength, they found Him. The first scout of the day shouted over his shoulder, "I found Him! He's over here! Hurry!" And with the scout in the lead, the swarm followed, eager for Jesus to begin unwrapping more mysteries of God.[5]

Jesus stepped closer and closer to the water, and the crowd followed suit. Jesus spied a boat, and beside it, its owner, washing out his fishing net at the end of his night's work.[6]

And so Jesus arrived in the life of a man named Simon.[7]

Of course he had to know Who Jesus was, since everyone did. And it wasn't as if he could ignore the mass that had intruded upon his beach and his work space. He had perhaps stood with his back to the crowd, straining to hear Jesus' teachings while busily staying on task so he could go home to bed. It had been a long and futile night on the job.[8] And at least listening to Jesus took his mind off his brother, Andrew's, gaze. He was no doubt just as unhappy to come in from a pointless night of work. The unspoken brother-spat hung heavily in the air.

And then Simon was aware that he was being addressed…by *Jesus*.

He looked up to find Jesus stepping near his boat – asking to use it.[9] *Jesus?* Use *his* boat? Simon couldn't scramble in quickly enough, dragging Andrew and the nets in with him.[10] He cleared a spot for Jesus and hastened to row out just a bit so Jesus was protected from the crowd, yet still able to speak easily to them.[11]

Simon Peter and Andrew dropped their nets and listened as Jesus taught. Who knows…perhaps hours passed and their own exhaustion from the long night evaporated until they barely remembered those miserable, fruitless hours. At last, Jesus' teaching ended, and whether the people scattered and went about their day's business or lurked persistently nearby, we do not know.[12]

But Jesus' focus shifted to the men whose boat He'd borrowed – Simon Peter in particular. He said, "Push out into deep water, and let your nets out for a catch."[13]

Simon Peter, known throughout the gospels for his typical rash speaking habits introduced himself to Jesus with a burst of expert fisherman opinion. "Master, we've worked hard all night and haven't caught anything. But because you say so, I will let down the nets."[14] Leave it to *Peter* to give Jesus the first impression of a lifetime. To inform Him of how hard they'd been working and how His suggestion really wouldn't help. Yet Peter agreed to do it anyway…out of courtesy.

It's a good thing Jesus could see past the shell and even the outer core of the heart, because that is one lousy first impression.[15]

Peter and Andrew (who probably turned his head to cover his reddened face after his brother's comment) dutifully rowed out to the usual fishing depth and lowered the nets.[16] Even as they expertly issued the nets over the sight of the boat, Peter no doubt mumbled under his breath, *Jesus is an amazing man when it comes to the Law, and he's a good speaker. I can see why people like to listen. But he really should leave this to those of us who know what we're doing. What am I going to say to him when nothing happens? He will be so embarrassed. I'm glad we're so far out here where everyone can't see him make a fool of himself.*

The sound of snapping string broke into Peter's silent monologue. What was that?

He glanced over the edge of the boat. Had they caught the net on the boat somehow? Oh if that net was ruined because of this crazy pointless mission…

…the fish! Oh the fish!! So many fish!! "Andrew!!" Peter threw his upper body over the boat and began to tug on the monstrous nets. He could barely reach the edge of them to hoist them inside the boat – the fish! They flipped and tossed and sank heavily into the bulging, breaking nets.[17]

The two muscular men…the two skillful fishermen…strained as never before while they wrestled with their nets. They began to shout, "James! John!" Their fishing partners were on shore alongside their father, Zebedee. They were going to need those three to come alongside with a second boat and more manpower.[18]

James and John rowed out to meet Simon Peter and Andrew. All four men gathered the snapping nets into the boats and found themselves with so many fish that the boats themselves began to sink into the water.[19]

As the water they rowed through every day threatened to spill over into the boats, Peter thought about his pious words. How he had looked this Man in the eye and tried to put Him in His place. How could he have been so stupid? How humiliating!

Simon Peter may have spoken hastily, but he did know how to try to make amends…though perhaps in an exaggerated fashion. Still, something had to be said. Turning to Jesus, who sat quietly in the end of the weighted boat, Peter exclaimed, "Go away from me, Lord; I am a sinful man!"[20]

Now where was Jesus supposed to go? He was in Peter's boat in the middle of a lake! Why had Peter said that? This had gone from bad to worse. But Jesus just *had* to know…*had* to understand that Peter saw how ridiculously he had acted. How stupid.

If only they could get this boat to shore, perhaps Jesus would climb out and be on His way and Peter would never have to see Him again. He could not bear it. To be with this Man was to be reminded of his thoughtless, impulsive self. This is why he was a fisherman. He could be brash when he worked with fish.

Even as he darted his gaze everywhere possible except up to meet Jesus' eyes, he felt those strong, gentle eyes staring straight at him.

At last he swallowed hard and looked at Jesus. He could not believe the words he heard:

Don't be afraid; from now on you will catch men.[21]

Don't be afraid. Jesus *knew.* He knew Peter hadn't meant it. He knew words had just spilled from his mouth before he had time to think about how they sounded. Jesus wasn't angry. And what was this? Jesus wanted Peter to *join* Him in His work? He wanted Peter to give up the occupation he'd always had and become part of this exciting new traveling ministry He was conducting?

Peter realized the invitation wasn't just for him...it was also for Andrew...and James...and John.[22]

Scripture says "they pulled their boats up on shore, left everything and followed him."[23] Other gospel accounts say that James and John even left their father Zebedee still in the boat.[24] They didn't take time to ponder... make lists...weigh options. They had seen a miracle of Jesus touch their own lives and to resist His invitation would have been as foolish as trying to tell Him that they knew how to fish better than He – the One Who made the fish.

When Jesus arrived, Peter made a fool of himself. But he found himself understood, forgiven, and offered a brand new path in life.

December 7

When the Lord saw her, his heart went out to her and he said, "Don't cry."
Luke 7:13

That day her only mission was to make it through the next second – only to find another second meeting her head-on. Then she started all over.

The woman did not look to the right or to the left. She could feel the presence of her friends...and of people she didn't even know. She knew they followed closely behind her, but she did not look to them. She looked only straight ahead.

When she looked straight ahead, she could see his hair. The hair she had combed with her fingers and cut carefully when it began to hang into his eyes. Today his hair fell to the side and she just now noticed it. Perhaps she resisted the urge to rush forward and move it back into place.

His friends bore the burden of his body slowly and cautiously.[1] Part of their meager pace stemmed from the shock that still overwhelmed them. He had been fine...and then gone. Soaked with life...and then denied it. Planning for his future...and then leaving his mother to plan for his funeral.[2]

What would she do? Middle aged, she was likely without a father or mother. She had probably walked behind a coffin three times before, leaving her orphaned and then widowed.[3] This boy had been her life – bringing joy to her tiny home in the days when the silence brought on by his father's death would have otherwise silenced her own heart.

This boy – this miniature version of the man she had loved – was her reason to live. Imagine her friends waving at her each night as they welcomed their husbands...and disappeared inside their homes for family dinners. She had no husband, but she did have the boy. The boy who in too short a time would have a home of his own. She would miss him. But he would care for her. And he would love her. She was sure of that.[4]

And now he was gone with no warning...no goodbye. To breathe hurt. To move took effort. To stare vacantly came naturally.

She felt the presence of the neighbors. The crowd had grown from what it was when her mother died...even more from when her father died...

and from the sound of the plodding, even more than when her precious husband died. The mourners increased with her mourning.[5]

But none of them mattered, really. The one that mattered was the lifeless one.

What would she do? She pushed away the thought. How could she even look ahead to that right now? No parents. No husband. No son. That equaled no hope. She would be forced to fall at the mercy of benevolent souls.[6] She hated that. She was able-bodied and full of life. Well, her soul was void of its life, but her body could function.

The caravan was slowing. Why? They were not to the tomb yet. The route she knew so instinctively now still had steps until the end. Why were they slowing?[7]

A man.

A young man.

A man not so many years different than her boy.[8] She couldn't even look him in the face. It was too much. Surely he could see that she had lost one just like him. She didn't even know him. Never mind that she didn't know several in the crowd pushing from behind. They at least stayed behind her. This one was walking straight toward her. Interrupting her son's funeral.

The tears she had been working to will away fell freely. How dare he! Did he not know her son? Never mind. Whether or not he knew him, this man should not presume to be welcome in this final walk.

Don't cry.[9]

She caught her breath. He spoke to her? She walked behind the coffin of her only son and last hope, on her way to leave him in a cold rock tomb[10] and this stranger dared to challenge her NOT to cry?

But Jesus had been touched.[11] As He walked along the road and saw the mournful procession creeping down the dusty street, He saw *her*. He knew, of course, because He was Jesus. But even if He weren't Jesus, He could have seen that this cold corpse had been her last hope. Her reason for life.

And perhaps in that moment He saw a moment just about three years away.[12] Another procession. Another heartbroken mother walking just steps behind her lifeless Son. As His own mother's face appeared in His mind, He knew He would want someone to have compassion on her that day.[13]

This woman needed compassion.

This woman needed Him.

He couldn't have missed the way she recoiled in confusion and anger when he gently urged her not to cry.

So Jesus moved into line with the grieving friends who bore the boy's body. They stopped and watched to see what He would do.[14]

Jesus stretched out His hand and touched the edge of the coffin. Before the sobbing mother could reach out to push Him away, He spoke. "Young man, I say to you, get up!"[15]

The mourners stilled, the bearers froze, and the mother trembled violently...staring at the coffin.

Was that movement? The boy's arms lifted from where they rested on his stomach, and he pulled himself into a sitting position. The thatch of hair fell right back into place and he rubbed his eyes.[16]

He began to speak...Where was he? What was happening? Why was everyone so sad? Who was this Man?[17]

Jesus reached for his hand and the boy hopped from the coffin bed.[18] It clapped to the ground where his astonished friends dropped it. Jesus led the boy to his mother where she collapsed into his arms, weeping.[19]

The air that had been filled with wailing and mourning was now filled with shouts of praise and exclamation.[20] Mourners threw aside their heavy veils and sackcloths and danced in the streets, marveling over the miracle they had seen.[21]

The woman did not seek Jesus' arrival that day. But Jesus arrived anyway. He restored all she had lost. He robbed death even as it had robbed life.

December 8

...and as she stood behind him at his feet weeping, she began to wet his feet with her tears. Then she wiped them with her hair, kissed them, and poured perfume on them.
Luke 7:38

She probably heard the news through the grapevine. The Pharisees were notorious for proclaiming their business. Their intention was for others to see and admire their obvious righteousness.[1] As a result, people usually knew what was happening in the world of the Pharisees.

This day, this Pharisee probably wished he'd kept his mouth shut about the dinner invitation he had extended to Jesus.[2] He'd only wanted everyone to know that *Jesus*, the Man of the moment had accepted his gesture. *Jesus* would dine with him. *Only* the very elite (and of course Jesus' traveling companions) would be allowed to attend.[3]

And as that information passed through the wagging whispers of the locals, *she* learned the news.[4]

We don't know much about her, but what we know is enough. She was a woman who had lived a sinful life. Tradition tells us that was probably code for prostitute.[5]

She may have seen Him before...as she hid near her corner, exposed by the daylight, knowing she would not be welcome at His teachings. Although the longer He talked, she began to wonder if just maybe He *would* welcome her. After all, He had said, "Do not judge, and you will not be judged. Do not condemn, and you will not be condemned. Forgive, and you will be forgiven. Give, and it will be given to you. A good measure, pressed down, shaken together and running over, will be poured into your lap. For with the measure you use, it will be measured to you."[6]

She probably thought a lot about that philosophy. She knew about being judged. She lived that every day. The disparaging looks – often cast to her by the very ones who visited her secretly after nightfall.

The freedom and forgiveness this Man spoke of – it seemed real. She had to know. She had to see for herself. But when?

And then she heard the buzz. *Jesus* would be at the home of the Pharisee.[7] Her heartbeat surely quickened. What if He never came this way again? What if this would be her only chance to meet Him?

Oh but how could she? She would never be allowed in the house. There would be important people there. Ones who would cast her back into the street before she even darkened the doorway.[8]

Maybe she could just wait outside and as He left…yes…maybe that would be the plan.

She heard the words again in her head…*Give, and it will be given to you. A good measure, pressed down, shaken together and running over will be poured into your lap.*[9]

Where did the woman get the money for the perfume she purchased? We do not know. Perhaps she ran home and went straight to the stash she had been keeping. Maybe for years, she had put away a bit at a time and it finally amounted to almost a year's earnings.[10] She hadn't really known why she was saving…she just saved.

Gathering up the money, she went into the marketplace and purchased a very expensive alabaster box filled with perfume.[11] She gave every penny and would have given more if she'd had it. Holding the treasure tightly against her, she made her way toward the Pharisee's house.

Perhaps she stood at a distance, and seeing no crowd or guard, she moved closer…closer…closer…until she could see inside the window. Jesus and the other guests were eating dinner and no one was watching the door.[12]

She couldn't stop herself…she just kept walking…walking.

She moved until she stood directly behind Jesus and then the tears came.[13] She wept hard, aware that she did not belong here. Aware of the scowls she received from the host…the guests…perhaps even Jesus' own friends.[14] But this was *Jesus*. Her eyes met His and He showed no scorn.

Give and it will be given to you.[15]

The woman fell and wept until Jesus' travel-dusted feet were soaked with her tears. She tried to compose herself but could not stop. Embarrassed, she began to dry His feet with the only thing she had – her long hair.[16] She was accustomed to using her hair to get the attention of men…letting it flow freely and openly when she should have it covered and tied.[17] But this time she wasn't aiming for attention or affection. She just wanted to show her adoration.[18]

Good measure pressed down, shaken together and running over.[19]

She kissed Jesus' feet and broke the alabaster box …pouring the perfume over Him.[20]

The woman did not even hear the Pharisee as he mumbled under his breath, "If this man were a prophet, he would know who is touching him and what kind of woman she is – that she is a sinner."[21]

But Jesus did know. He knew this woman had paid dearly to meet Him. She had risked safety, embarrassment, and paid a dear monetary price for this moment. He saw her heart. Her ache to be free from her sinful life. Her desire to know she wasn't judged. Her act of love.

He turned to the Pharisee and said, "Do you see this woman? I came into your house. You did not give me any water for my feet, but she wet my feet with her tears and wiped them with her hair. You did not give me a kiss, but this woman, from the time I entered, has not stopped kissing my feet. You did not put oil on my head, but she has poured perfume on my feet. Therefore, I tell you, her many sins have been forgiven – for she loved much. But he who has been forgiven little loves little."[22]

…will be poured into your lap.[23]

The woman drank in Jesus' words as though they were perfume poured over her.

Jesus was real. The words she'd heard Him say earlier…He meant. He lived.

Jesus was understanding. He knew her motive. He saw her need without a word spoken.

Jesus loved. He addressed her personally as more tears cascaded down her face: "Your faith has saved you; go in peace."[24]

Her heart rejoiced. She may have lost every bit of her savings, but He had saved her.

Jesus arrived and He gave her peace in exchange for her life of sin.

She was free.

December 9

Jesus asked him, "What is your name?" "Legion," he replied, because many demons had gone into him.
Luke 8:30

If we were to ask the man about the moment Jesus arrived, chances are he wouldn't even remember. He was there, but his mind belonged to the twisted control of an entire host of demons.[1] Only they would remember that day.

Jesus had just stepped from a sailboat when the man met him.[2] He was wild man in appearance and action – naked and probably caked with filth from every conceivable source. His hair was long and matted and his beard hid everything but the evil glint in his dark eyes.[3] No one would have dared to go near him – he danced around growling and yelling and running from one tomb to the next. The only people who would give him a home were the dead; they couldn't drive him away.[4]

What brought him away from the tombs that day? Why did he wander from the dark dampness where the demons held him captive? We can't be sure what lured him.

The man may not have known the Man in front of him, but the demons knew.[5] And though they dwelled in this man and forced him to create fear among the people, that day they were the ones who felt the fear.

"What do you want with me, Jesus, Son of the Most High God? I beg you, don't torture me!"[6]

Even the demons respected Jesus enough to know they were at His mercy. The man in whose body they lived simply fell to the ground as they shouted through him.[7] Perhaps it was a blessing he wasn't aware of his surroundings.

Jesus asked the man his name and the demons answered "Legion."[8] Many of them fought for control of the wild and naked man – each torturing him more than the last. He may have writhed on the ground as the demons twisted in turmoil within him – awaiting their fate to be issued by Jesus.

Perhaps they had done a better job with this man than most. They had infested him until he had to be chained. Then they continued to torture him until not even chains and guards could confine him. They had driven him to the tombs and kept him there to dwell among the dead.[9] Until that day.

He was at their mercy.

And now all of them were at the mercy of Jesus.

Jesus' heart swelled with compassion at the man perhaps not much different in age from Himself. One who could boast such a full life…if only he could be freed to live it.

The demons must have known their time in the man was limited. They knew Jesus' heart enough to know He would not let the man suffer any longer. So they did the only thing they could – they begged for mercy for themselves.[10]

They knew about the abyss. It was the place where their master Satan and all his evil spirits were confined.[11] A dark and sin-infested place – so evil, they feared even the thought of it. So they begged Jesus to relocate them to a nearby herd of pigs.[12] At least there they could continue their control, even if it was a demotion from controlling a person.

We don't know what Jesus said – if there was a quiet command or a great display, but Jesus spoke.[13] The man was stilled even as the herd of pigs, now possessed by the legion of demons, suddenly stormed down a steep bank and drowned in the river.[14]

Imagine the man – awakening on the shore – lying very still – looking to the right and the left, trying to determine where he was…*who* he was.

He looked up and saw a kind face with gentle eyes leaning over him. Did he know it was Jesus? Did the exodus of demons wipe his entire memory of the months they lived in him? Or did he well remember their torture of him? Did he realize he was looking into the eyes of the Man who gave him life? Did he know he was meeting *Jesus*?

We don't know. Surely he sat up and realized his nakedness even as Jesus provided a garment for him to wear – perhaps a piece of His own clothing pulled from His very shoulders.[15]

Jesus may have sent him to the river to clean his filthy body and hair so when people began to arrive to investigate the mass suicide of the swine, they would find truly a different man than the naked wild monster who lived in the tombs.[16]

The man hastened to clean up so he could sit with Jesus and learn from Him. Thank Him profusely. Find out how to live a normal life.

Jesus and the man sat on the shore…speaking Man to man. The first onlookers arrived – led by the pig-herders in search of their missing charges – or at least an explanation of the missing swine.[17]

Perhaps the people weren't sure what shocked them more. The dead pigs or the reformed crazy man who was inexplicably normal.

And though the man drank in everything that Jesus was, the people could not. They were not ready to accept this level of holiness…of change… of healing. They only knew when this Man stepped on shore, pigs drowned and crazy men became as one of them.

In pure fear, they begged Jesus to leave.[18]

Jesus, never One to force His presence upon anyone, quietly got into the boat and prepared to leave their presence.[19]

The man ran behind…into the water…reaching for the end of the boat. He begged Jesus to be allowed to follow along. He had nothing to go back to. No home. No clothes. No family. No job. No friends. Why should he stay?[20]

But Jesus requested him to stay. "Return home and tell how much God has done for you."[21]

Though surely disappointed, the man was eager to complete his assignment from God. Not just anyone had a story quite that grand, and meeting Jesus left him eager to share his story of deliverance. A missionary appointed by the Master Himself.[22]

He had no formal training. No degree in public speaking or graduate work in divinity. But he had a story to tell – and he went away from Jesus and did just that. He left the dead in body and moved to the dead in spirit. All over town he went, telling all he met about a Man he met.[23]

Jesus' arrival was too good to keep quiet.

December 10

Then the woman, seeing that she could not go unnoticed, came trembling and fell at his feet. In the presence of all the people, she told why she had touched him and how she had been instantly healed.
Luke 8:47

She hadn't intended to actually meet Jesus. In a city where star-struck stalkers ran rampant, she was content to stay invisible.

Actually she just longed to *be* invisible.

For twelve years, this woman had lived with what might as well have been a flashing sign attached to her forehead. She bled. It was that simple. For twelve long years she awoke each day to find fresh blood coming from within her.[1]

If it were to happen to any of us, we would consider it annoying.

For this woman it was life-altering. Crushing, in fact. For in her day, to bleed from anywhere for any reason made a person unclean.[2] And the unclean had no place in society. She had no place. After twelve years, she probably also had no *one*. Her family had long given up on her. They had lives to live and couldn't wait around for her to get better.

Had she lost a husband? Perhaps she had children, but she'd missed most of their lives because they couldn't be near her. If anyone had touched her – even accidentally – they too would be considered unclean by association.[3]

She couldn't ask that of her family, her friends. So she lived in seclusion. Seclusion was lonely, but preferable to the alternative. Anytime she wanted to go somewhere, she had to announce her presence in a loud voice as she moved through the streets.[4]

Unclean! Unclean!

People scattered as though to breathe her air would bring final breaths upon them. They cast annoying glares her direction, irritated that her mere presence in the street required relocation for them. Mothers instinctively grabbed their children and pulled them to the side until she passed. She ignored their not-so-subtle whispers, knowing full well they were explaining to the little ones why she was a terrifying person who warranted avoidance.

Twelve years later, she thought she should be past the part where tears stung her eyes during those moments, but she still felt them. Her heart felt the barbs of pain too.

She had heard of this Jesus. She had heard of water becoming wine[5] and lepers becoming clean[6] and demons leaving the possessed.[7] If only there was a way to get to Him.

But there wasn't – and she needed to stop "if only-ing." She couldn't meet Him. She, a woman[8]...an *unclean* woman at that...could not approach the great Teacher and explain her predicament. Besides, she had heard He often touched those He healed. She couldn't ask Him to touch her. He would have to serve a period of being unclean, and she couldn't do that to Him. People would stone her to death if she became the reason He had to vanish into seclusion even for a time.[9]

But the day she heard He was coming into town...she bit her lip in wonder. Could it work? Everyone would be out. If she touched anyone... oh it would be awful. And how could she *not* touch someone? The crowd would be pressed tightly together.

Then it occurred to her that this really was the perfect opportunity. There *would* be a crowd. She could worm her way through and just touch the very edge of His clothing. Just the hem – right at the bottom – by His feet.[10] She knew it would be enough. The power was in His clothing as surely as it was in His body. It had to be. No one would have to know she was there and by the time she left Him, she would be healed and she could walk freely among the people.

The relief was so close she could feel it. She imagined going from that place and meeting her family and friends. Going to the doctors who had been unable to help her in any way and saying to them, "Look at me! I'm healed!"[11]

The day arrived and so did the crowds. The woman donned her most covering clothing and began to slip through the crowds. Out of respect, she avoided as many people as she could, but she did bump into a few here and there. She hurried past, biting her tongue from the instinct that usually voiced "Unclean!"

Jesus was moving in a hurry. She had heard a bit of a rumor that He was on His way to touch a dying girl.[12] She would have to move fast to catch Him. She neared the back of Him, reached out and caught the hem of His garment.[13] It was more of a flitting touch than a catch. But it was enough. She knew the last ounce of blood had left her body and she was healed.[14]

Poised to slip back into oblivion, the unthinkable happened. Just as she felt the last drop of blood leave her, He felt a drop of healing power leave Him. Jesus stopped, turned around, and asked, "Who touched my clothes?"[15]

The woman's eyes slid shut and her shoulders slumped in defeat. She could sense the crowd stirring – looking around – wondering who Jesus could have meant by His questions. After all – dozens crowded around. What could she say? She had broken the custom by not announcing her uncleanness and she had stolen a healing from Jesus.

She hadn't intended to really meet Him. She only intended to take what He offered.

But she learned you can't take what He offers without meeting Him.

The woman, shaking in fear, moved toward Him and admitted her story. Through tears and nagging trepidation, she told the whole thing from beginning to end.[16] Those around who recognized her cleared away, leaving her alone with Jesus in a circle of avoidance.

Jesus looked at her and said, "Daughter, your faith has healed you. Go in peace."[17]

It wasn't the clothing after all. It was her faith. That was what healed her. And He wasn't angry. He wasn't yelling at her. He wasn't signing up to be unclean for the required time.

And that word resounded...*Daughter.*

How long had it been since anyone claimed her as anything other than the town freak?

The spotlight left her just then, because word came that the dying girl he was on His way to see had in fact, just died.[18] The focus became about her and her father, the dignitary.

The crowd moved on, but the woman stayed back.

Daughter...she arrived looking for healing, but Jesus arrived and brought about acceptance.

Your faith...Jesus' arrival taught her what she had was what she needed.

Has healed you...Jesus' arrival met her deepest need.

Go in peace...Jesus' arrival released her to be whole.

December 11

And he took the children in his arms, put his hands on the, and blessed them.
Mark 10:16

They were just children – some maybe even infants. No doubt very few of them remembered that particular day.[1]

But just maybe a few did. They would have sensed their parents' excitement – the hurry and rush to get the day started. The extra attention given to smoothing out the same play-dirtied garments they wore every day. The additional spit-bath applied to the stubborn cowlicks of hair.

And then they were ushered out into the street and toward the crowd. The kids wanted to run freely in the street playing with their friends as they always did. But today their parents had other plans. Plans that included this crowd.[2]

They couldn't see anything. They were too short. And the people behind them were just as eager as their parents. They pushed hard, smashing the little children into their parents' sides.

Up ahead, they could hear a man talking – but His words made no sense. They heard something about divorce and what God joined, let man not separate…but what is divorce? Who is God? What is He joining?[3]

The children clung tightly to their parents' hands and stumbled along behind them, tripping over stones in the dirt street. What was the big hurry?

They guessed they were near the destination, because the Man speaking was at last within earshot, and for some of the taller ones, maybe even within sight. He wasn't anyone particularly amazing, at least in looks, but there was just something about Him that captivated even the smallest eyes.[4] Was it the twinkle in His own? Or the smile? The gentle roll of His voice? Or just the kind welcome that seemed to surround His entire Being?

The children heard their parents asking for this Man to touch the children – just even to pat their heads or the tips of their hands.[5] Why would He need to do that? Maybe some child vaguely remembered hearing parental whispers in the darkness after she was supposed to be asleep… whispers of "His touch heals so many. Maybe if He touches just the top of her head now, it will keep her from becoming sick." Was this the Man from the conversation? Was that true? If He touched her, would that mean she never again would have a cold or skinned up-knees?

But even as the parents pulled their children closer to Jesus, His friends began to create a barricade between Him and them.[6] They insisted Jesus had more important things to do right then. He had much to do, in fact, and could not be bothered by noisy, dirty children. They were only interruptions to the day.

Those children who had the ability to remember probably had the next moment ingrained in their minds until their dying days.

Jesus rose up, and though He didn't frighten the children, His voice was firm and a steely glint crept into His eye. He looked directly at the men called disciples – His own friends and spoke sternly: "Let the little children come to me, and do not hinder them, for the kingdom of God belongs to such as these."[7]

The men stepped back and the children broke free from their parents' holds on their tiny arms. Curiosity mixed with glee and the children rushed at the Man Jesus who knelt down to meet them at eye level. His arms spread open wide and the children threw their own arms around His neck and nearly knocked Him to the ground with their hugs.

Jesus kept speaking: "I tell you the truth, anyone who will not receive the kingdom of God like a little child will never enter it."[8]

They may not have known what the kingdom of God meant, but they knew this Man loved them. They were not aware that He even knew them, and yet they knew He loved them. He might have asked their names and listened as they told stories of their latest adventures at play in the streets with their neighbors and siblings. He patiently answered their myriad of questions about Who He was and why the men tried to push everyone away from Him. Some brave soul may have even asked what the kingdom of God was and how to get there.

Parents stood in awe as Jesus met their children. He ran around the grassy knoll with them, played their silly little made-up games, kissed away boo-boos and laughed at their antics. He let them climb all over Him and shower Him with hugs and trivial information that just burst to escape their tiny minds.

They were just children. They had no voice in society, they made no contribution to the economy, but they meant everything to His Message. The unabashed energy, the shameless enthusiasm, the pointed affection they showered upon Him – oh if only their parents could be so free!

Whether He spent just a few moments with them or several hours, their time together did come to an end. Jesus explained He must be on His way, but before He left, He gathered them each in His arms once more and blessed them.[9]

Not a magical blessing to keep away all illness for all time, but a blessing of life – a blessing from God Himself – was poured over each child. Tiny eyes gazed widely into His, perhaps not understanding quite what was happening, but comprehending enough to know that it was very important.

And so Jesus arrived to the tiniest audience. They had just met Life in the beginning of their own young lives. They had been blessed by the One Whose blessing surpasses all other blessings.

Maybe many years later, those same children met other men. Men named Paul[10] and Barnabas[11] and Timothy.[12] Men who were pillars in a group called Believers.[13] They spoke of a Man Whose life was the pattern for all others to follow.[14]

And as these children, who were now the parents of their own children, listened to the words, perhaps they remembered a day half a lifetime ago, when they ran across a field and into the arms of a Man whose kind eyes invited them in. They might have remembered the pressure of His hand on their heads as He blessed them.

Maybe those words...*let the little children come...do not hinder them... the kingdom of God belongs to such as these...*[15] came back to them as they looked down into the wide, wondering eyes of their own children... and they knew that they had encountered something and Someone very special.

The Man was not there any longer in bodily form to offer the same blessing over their children, but *they* could bless them by offering their lives as living sacrifices, holy and pleasing to the God[16] who had blessed them and then offered Himself as a sacrifice.[17]

December 12

Then Jesus declared, "I who speak to you am he."
John 4:26

What was the Samaritan woman thinking as she walked toward the well? Did she even see outside the narrow walls of her mind's world to notice there was a man resting at the well?[1]

She probably was so intent on hastening to the well, getting the water she needed, and hurrying back home before anyone arrived, she didn't even see Jesus sitting there.[2]

It was a little game she played every day of her life – the game of survival – and the successful days were the ones when she didn't have to speak to anyone. No one liked her anyway. She was a tramp and everyone knew it. Long ago, after the first failed marriage, she had hoped to make something of her life. But after the third one, she gave up. From then on, she just moved from one man to the next, taking whatever she could get – and giving whatever he required. What was the point in changing?[3]

When she finally did notice someone at the well, she realized he was a Jew. Great. What could be worse than the righteous women of the community finding her there? A Jewish man finding her. Jews hated Samaritans.[4] And men didn't address women unless they wanted something. That was exactly how she'd gotten the reputation she had. She silently begged this man to keep his mouth shut. She didn't need another proposition.

"Will you give me a drink?"[5]

Not the words she had expected to hear. But maybe this was some sort of game he played to bait his women. Okay, she would play along.

"You are a Jew and I am a Samaritan woman. How can you ask me for a drink?"[6] There. That should silence him.

"If you knew the gift of God and who it is that asks you for a drink, you would have asked him and he would have given you living water."[7]

She wasn't accustomed to thinking so hard with these word games. What was he talking about? She didn't have time to figure it out. If she didn't hurry, a townswoman would show up and if any upright woman found her there talking to a foreign man…well…she might lose her latest catch, who was waiting for her at home. Even if he wasn't much of a catch, she needed him.[8]

"Sir, you have nothing to draw with and the well is deep."[9] She looked at him pointedly, her tone conveying that this little conversation had already ceased to amuse her. "Where can you get this living water? Are you greater than our father Jacob, who gave us the well and drank from it himself, as did also his sons and his flocks and herds?"[10]

There. At least if he viewed her only as a target, he would know she was a target with a measure of brains. At least she knew her well history. Hopefully she had put him in his place.

"Everyone who drinks this water will be thirsty again, but whoever drinks the water I give him will never thirst. Indeed, the water I give him will become in him a spring of water welling up to eternal life."[11]

The woman stopped and pondered that for a moment. Maybe he wasn't playing a game. She knew at least the first part was true. She drank from this well every day – and yet every day that followed, she was thirsty again. Could this man give her something that would allow her to avoid this dismal run to the well every day? Could she avoid the disapproving stares of the women?

Before she could stop herself, she blurted out, "Sir, give me this water so that I won't get thirsty and have to keep coming here to draw water."[12]

Already she could feel hope surging – this man had the answer! She knew it!

"Go, call your husband and come back."[13]

What? What was he talking about? Oh – maybe it was a property issue, and he couldn't just tell her. He might need a man there.[14] Oh she hated to tell him – but she had no reason to lie.

"I have no husband."[15]

"You are right when you say you have no husband. The fact is, you have had five husbands, and the man you have now is not your husband. What you have just said is quite true."[16]

All color drained from her face and she grabbed onto the side of the well to steady herself. How could he have possibly known that about her? I mean even if he had been around town for a day or two to know she was a woman of reputation, he couldn't have known that much detail. The stories about her, after all, had grown until she had been with thirty men, if you heard it from any of the townspeople. But this Man! He knew it all!

And yet…He was factual. Not condemning. The women who didn't even *know* the truth pursed their lips at the mere sight of her. And yet this Man – He continued to speak to her like she had worth.

"Sir, I can see that you are a prophet. Our fathers worshiped on this mountain, but you Jews proclaim that the place where we must worship is in Jerusalem."[17]

She didn't know much more than that, but He was obviously an important man in disguise and she needed Him to know she wasn't stupid – just riddled with poor choices.

"Believe me, woman, a time is coming when you will worship the Father neither on this mountain nor in Jerusalem. You Samaritans worship what you do not know; we worship what we do know, for salvation is from the Jews. Yet a time is coming and has now come when the true worshipers will worship the Father in spirit and truth, for they are the kind of worshipers the Father seeks. God is spirit and his worshipers must worship in spirit and in truth."[18]

Never had a man spoken with her so boldly and so respectfully. Never had one spoken to her mind at all – only to her body. And yet how did her heart feel so tenderly loved compared to all the men she had known?

In a mere whisper she said, "I know that the Messiah is coming. When he comes, he will explain everything to us."[19]

Though she had never told anyone, she ached for that day. She wanted to know more.

"I who speak to you am he."[20]

The Master had arrived. She, a woman of reputation…a woman whose life had been trashed by her own poor choices…a woman who lived even that day in blatant sin…met Jesus. And Jesus, through pure conversation, transformed a tramp into a lady. He showed her the worth the Father had created her to possess. The worth of a mind. The worth of decency. The worth of pure attention.

She had hastened to the well to get the water she needed and planned to hurry home. She received the Water she needed and she did hurry home…to a new life. She told everyone she met, "Come, see a man who told me everything I ever did. Could this be the Christ?"[21]

And she knew He *was* indeed the Christ.

December 13

When Jesus reached the spot, he looked up and said to him, "Zacchaeus, come down immediately. I must stay at your house today."
Luke 19:5

Zacchaeus had it all by Jericho standards.[1] He had a steady job, and at that, a job that paid him well. And in those moments when he didn't feel like it paid enough, he helped himself to a little more on the side and then it did indeed pay enough – and more. He had worked his way to the top of the tax collector world and the young hopefuls sought his advice on how to get to the top, no matter the cost.[2]

If there had been seminars available in that day, Zacchaeus would have been the keynote speaker. He had started early, watched the best in action, and he *became* the best.[3] Granted, he wasn't the most popular among the working class.[4] But then Zacchaeus didn't really care about the working class. If they would only work a little harder, they could be as good as he. But they didn't work harder. So they deserved whatever they got…or rather, whatever he gave or took from them.[5]

Why did Zacchaeus want to see Jesus so much? Maybe it irritated him that this new person in town seemed to be stealing some of the limelight Zacchaeus tried so hard to gain for himself. Or perhaps he wondered if maybe…just maybe…this man might know the one thing he didn't know – which was how to fill up that nagging ache of emptiness that he felt somewhere *so* deep inside he wasn't even sure how to access it.

He had heard Jesus would be passing through the town that day. He wasn't stopping to do his traditional teaching, but he would at least be going by.[6] That was the word circulating through the crowds who were in a hurry to pay their taxes that day so they could get out with the rest of the people to see the renowned Jesus.[7]

Zacchaeus wasn't one to close up shop early – that might cost him too much money – and any money lost was too much money. But curiosity overcame greed for just a moment, and he left his post to catch a glimpse of the celebrity passing through.[8]

And that is where his one shortcoming presented a problem. The shortcoming was just that – he was short.[9] In the business world, his temper and determination had always made up for his lack of threatening height. But in the regular world, those he cheated in taxes cheated him right back, crowding around him and preventing him from being able to see anything.

Usually he just turned red in the face and stomped home.

That day he felt compelled to press on. He had to see Jesus.[10]

He tried asking nicely to be excused. No one paid attention.

He tried pushing. People pushed back.

He tried yelling, but his voice was drowned by the shouts and cheers and questions of those who lined the streets. No one saw him. That day he wasn't the dreaded tax collector. That day he was just a short nobody.

As he stepped to the side and started to inwardly admit his defeat, he looked ahead and saw it. A sycamore-fig tree.[11] It had been years since he climbed a tree. In fact, he'd been a boy last time he attempted such a stunt. And given his overabundance of wine and fine dinners in the past few years, any sort of physical activity would leave him straining for breath. But this tree...it had a thick trunk and branches that started down low. It was a sturdy looking tree. Maybe it would just do the trick.

Zacchaeus ran ahead and began to pull and climb up and out the branches of the tree.[12] It wasn't a very tall tree, but the branch he found made him just tall enough that he could see over the crowd. He perched as comfortably as he could and waited.

The din grew louder, telling him that Jesus was getting closer. Zacchaeus leaned forward, just hoping to see what His face looked like. That was all.[13]

Jesus walked through, smiling, waving...and yet not in an attention-drawing sort of way. It was all very genuine. *Genuine.* How did Zacchaeus even know the meaning of that word?

Even as he sorted it all out in his head, he became aware that everyone was staring right at him. They stood, faces upturned, looking into the tree, and Zacchaeus became embarrassed. There he was, a dignified business man, sitting in a tree! And yet before he could think another word, Jesus spoke – to him! "Zacchaeus, come down immediately. I must stay at your house today."[14]

How did Jesus know who he was? How did He know his name? But what was that last part? Jesus wanted to come over? To his house? To be a guest? To eat dinner? To stay? For how long?

Why would Jesus want to do that?? *Why?*

Even as Zacchaeus scrambled down from his perch in the tree,[15] he could not ignore the murmurings of the people. "He has gone to be the guest of a 'sinner.'"[16]

Why did that word sting so much? He had been called so many things. He had stood by while grown men shook their fists, threw objects, and spoke in ways they couldn't in front of the children, and women cried and begged – yet none of it even made him flinch.

But to be called a *sinner*.

To meet the Master.

He was filthy and he knew it.

He welcomed Jesus to his home[17] and before Jesus had even been there very long, Zacchaeus said to Him, "Look, Lord! Here and now I give half of my possessions to the poor, and if I have cheated anybody out of anything, I will pay back four times the amount."[18]

Zacchaeus looked around and realized all his wealth – all his fine possessions – all his money in the bank – meant nothing. He had amassed it illegitimately and it he deserved to lose it all. More than that, the people deserved to get it all back – with interest. With the same ridiculous interest rate he had charged them.

His servants stared in disbelief. What had happened to their dictator of a master? Who was this Man and what had He done to make Zacchaeus say such things?

But Jesus was speaking: "Today, salvation has come to this house, because this man, too, is a son of Abraham. For the Son of Man came to seek and to save what was lost."[19]

And just as the Son of Man came to seek what was lost, the lost sought the Son of Man that day. And in the arrival of the Son of Man, he was saved.

December 14

At this the man's face fell. He went away sad, because he had great wealth.
Mark 10:22

Matthew's account of this story tells us the man was *young*.[1] Luke calls him a *ruler*.[2] We can only guess his age to be old enough to hold a position of authority, yet young enough to still lack the life wisdom that only comes with age and experience.

Perhaps he was fascinated by Jesus' ministry and genuinely desired to become an apprentice of sorts so that he too could have such a vibrant career among the masses. Maybe he wanted the secret to life's biggest question condensed in such a way that he could market the information and become richer than he was already. Or someone else may have pondered the question, but because this young man was the ruler with the least seniority, he was the one sent to gather the information.

Whatever his motive, he approached Jesus with a syrupy sort of respect. He fell to his knees in front of Jesus and said, "Good teacher, what must I do to inherit eternal life?"[3] Maybe his superiors were hiding in the scattered groups of onlookers and he wanted to make a good impression. Or he might have learned from shadowing the ever scene-making leaders that to flatter the information-holder is always a good idea.

The man knew what he was after…and he had no doubt heard that if you ask, it will be given to you.[4] Even as the words poured from his mouth, he must have envisioned the bestowment of eternal life scratched on a parchment scroll. In his mind, the will of the Father physically mirrored the will of his earthly father.

Jesus didn't pull out any parchment to enter the man into Heaven, though. He reached out to pull the man to his feet, and said, "Why do you call me good? No one is good – except God alone."[5] Jesus – never fooled by flattery – wanted to make sure the man's focus was fixed securely on God the Father. Jesus knew He was the local celebrity, at least that day. He never wanted anyone to confuse faith with obsession in Him.

The man still stood – his question unanswered. Jesus knew that anyone the age and position of this man would be schooled in matters of spiritual law. He said, "You know the commandments: 'Do not murder, do not commit adultery, do not steal, do not give false testimony, do not defraud, honor your father and mother.'"[6]

The young man nodded eagerly with each addition to the lists. He knew about lists. He'd memorized list upon list of the Jewish law when he studied as a scholar in the Temple. In fact, for several years, that was *all* he had done. Memorize the lists and meticulously uphold each piece.[7] His face shone radiantly when Jesus stopped listing the major points of the law.

You see, this man had not just memorized the lists. He was an honor student. Eager to share his success with the Good Teacher, he said, "all these I have kept since I was a boy."[8]

Finally! All those years of being good when being bad seemed so tempting had finally paid off. There he stood, before the admired Teacher, able to proclaim that he had flawlessly observed everything that was needed to gain eternal life! Imagine his joy to be able to spread that word to his colleagues! They had been right in all they learned and subsequently taught those who came behind. It was about the rules!

Jesus didn't miss his enthusiasm. He didn't miss the look of relief on the man's face as he comprehended that he had done it right. The way the man bit his lip in an effort to restrain his joy did not escape Jesus' notice. And even though Jesus knew His next words would leave the man crestfallen in countenance and soul, *He loved this man.*[9]

This young, eager man before Him was one of the lost souls Jesus had come to save,[10] and more than Jesus could want rest or food at that moment, He wanted this man to understand the depth and truth of the Message of God.

With the look of love that could shine only from Jesus' eyes, He looked at the man and said, "One thing you lack. Go, sell everything you have and give to the poor, and you will have treasure in heaven. Then come, follow me."[11]

Scripture does not say the man uttered another word. Just simply "the man's face fell. He went away sad, because he had great wealth."[12]

Though Jesus' had not said these words to humiliate the young man, his ego was bruised to know he lacked anything at all. Jesus had just offered him the greatest bit of constructive criticism he could ever hope to gain. The man asked what he needed and Jesus told him specifically what was missing from his life. He told him so he could gain what he lacked. But the man couldn't get past the truth that *he lacked.*

From where the man stood, he had done everything right his whole life, and all Jesus could see was the one thing he couldn't do. From where

Jesus stood, it didn't matter that he'd done everything right his whole life, if he was unwilling to do the one thing that remained.

Jesus' mission wasn't to turn the population of the world into paupers who were sinners if they had any material possession. Jesus was reading into the man's heart. He had great wealth.[13] Perhaps part of it had been passed down through the family. Maybe a great chunk of it was the result of his own hard work at the start of his young career. But regardless of how he acquired it, he was addicted to it.[14]

Jesus knew the man was so devoted to his home, his possessions, and his position, that he would not be able to give them up for a life of uncertainty. His faith rested in what he had, not Who he had.[15] To give it up, to give it away, and to walk away...those were three things. Jesus said he lacked *one* thing. That one thing was full devotion. To give it up, give it away, and walk away would demonstrate his devotion.[16]

The man met Jesus that day hoping for an easy answer. The answer was easy in diagnosis. It was not easy in recovery.

The man met Jesus and instead of being handed a reward, he was handed a choice. And he chose to walk away. His heart broke. He purposefully walked away from eternal life. His heart *should* have broken.

Scripture doesn't say, but Jesus must have felt a tear well in His own eye as the man walked away, head down low. He didn't cease to love the man, but His heart ached at the choice made deliberately in front of Him. He simply looked at his disciples who had silently witnessed the exchange, and He said, "How hard it is for the rich to enter the kingdom of God!"[17]

Jesus arrived and offered the man a choice. A choice not unlike the one offered to each of us now.

December 15

...So taking hold of the man, he healed him and sent him away.
Luke 14:4b

Imagine a Sunday, Pharisee-style. Well, in that day, it was really Saturday,[1] but it was still the Sabbath day. The day of rest.[2] Pharisees took their Sabbaths very seriously. Not because they had any particular haste to refresh their minds and bodies for another week of service to the Lord, but more because the Sabbath provided them with another opportunity to show their righteousness to the surrounding community.[3]

No doubt the day began with a visit to the Temple. Skipping church just could not be allowed. The families paraded through the streets, dressed in their finest garments, cleansed and polished, moving along in a stately manner. Children seen and not heard, wife carefully in submission behind her husband. The perfect little family – moving in a picturesque line toward the Temple.[4]

After accomplishing a successful time at the Temple, the family parade returned home for a meal – carefully prepared the day before, of course, since no work was permitted on the Sabbath.[5] Once all appetites had been satisfied, the day was theirs to rest – to show those around what the righteous do – or do *not* do – on the Sabbath.

This particular Sabbath was not just *any* Sabbath for one Pharisee. He was one of the elite.[6] The highest ranking. The most respected – or was it the most envied? This day, he had managed to get *Jesus* to accept an invitation for a meal at his very home.[7] Jesus was always on the go – always traveling about, city to city. Always spending his time with the likes of those the Pharisees couldn't quite figure out.[8] They were certainly not holy. Definitely not righteous. And way behind on offerings at the Temple.[9]

He had probably been telling the other Pharisees for days about the preparation underway at his house. The cleaning. The bringing out of the very best. The borrowing of what just hadn't made it into his own personal collection yet. The new clothing. The extra attention to detail on the menu – a tricky one, since preparation had to be done a day ahead. And yet this time above all other times, there could be no cheating on the meal. How could he prove his meticulous righteousness to the great Jesus if his servants cheated on the meal preparation in His very presence?

In fact, if he were to be truthful, the Pharisee would have to admit that not only did he want to prove his righteousness to Jesus, but perhaps he'd be just lucky enough to be the one to cause Jesus Himself to stumble a bit in that department.[10] The man and his fellow Pharisees had been talking about this Man, Jesus, and there was just something strange in the air. He was *too* good. Somewhere in there, a flaw *must* be hiding. What if he became the one who managed to uncover it?

The Pharisee was ready to meet and impress Jesus, but the meeting of meetings that day was reserved for another man.

A "least of these" in the eyes of the Pharisee.[11]

The family parade was on its way home, and the prominent man led the way. He was aware of the eyes of his colleagues watching from the sides of the street and the distance of the Temple courts.[12] Were they jealous because he was the one Jesus agreed to eat with, or curious to see if he could uncover the mysteriousness that made up this Man?

He was so deep in thought, he barely saw the man in front of him.[13]

But Jesus saw him.

The man was not whole. He was afflicted with dropsy.[14] Maybe he had ventured outside the house that day only because it was the Sabbath and he wanted to honor the Lord in spite of the agony it caused him to make the journey from his home to the Temple. Maybe he had been bedridden for a few days and simply wanted to get some fresh air and sunshine to boost his spirits. Maybe he was on his way to the home of a friend who had offered him a meal so he wouldn't have to worry about finding something to eat on his own.

Whatever his reason for being in the street that, day, he found himself in the path of Jesus. And not just in His path – in His compassion.

Scripture does not indicate that the man spoke to Jesus at all. It doesn't say he knew Who Jesus was or that he cried out in a loud voice begging for healing. Perhaps the man did nothing at all but stand there and try to focus on the words he heard over the pain he felt.[15]

In fact, Jesus didn't address the man at all. He turned instead to his host and the other Pharisees who lurked nearby. "Is it lawful to heal on the Sabbath or not?"[16]

It was a trick question.

But even as the Pharisees tried to determine what to do or say, the man's world began to change. He stood there, not caring whether or not it was lawful. Pain wracked every inch of his body and the swelling stretched his skin until he thought he might burst. Would this Man – *could* this Man – fix him? Was this some sort of cruel joke?

Perhaps he *should* listen to the answer the Pharisees gave. If they told Jesus it wasn't lawful, he could just imagine Jesus nodding in agreement, congratulating them on the correct answer and the whole parade of them moving on to the Pharisee's house for lunch. Meanwhile, he would be left standing in the street, suffering more than before – for in addition to the pain, he would have an afflicted spirit as well.

No one spoke. Not one Pharisee had an answer to Jesus' question.[17] They just stood and stared. Jesus reached out, touched the man, and immediately the swelling subsided. The pain evaporated. His skin no longer stretched miserably until he couldn't bend.[18] He twisted one way and then the other. He felt young and healthy. He wanted to jump and run and scream with joy…but this was the middle of the street and it was the Sabbath.

How could he thank this Man? He knew he had merely been an illustration from the Great Teacher to the self-righteous leaders, but he didn't care. He had been healed in the process! What could he say? What could he do?

Jesus sent him away.[19] To Jesus, this man hadn't just been an illustration. He was a hurting soul and Jesus had the power to remove the hurt. Jesus didn't care what day it was or where they stood or anything else. He simply wanted to help the man. He had more to say to the Pharisees[20] who still stared in a combination of awe and anger, but it wasn't for the man to hear. The man needed to get on with his day – on with his life.

So Jesus sent him away. Such a brief meeting – but such a life changing one. The man had been a means of teaching, yes. But Jesus' arrival made him more than a teaching example. It made him whole.[21]

December 16

When Jesus saw him lying there and learned that he had been in this condition for a long time, he asked him, "Do you want to get well?"
John 5:6

The pool had probably once been a very beautiful place. A place of rest and rejuvenation.[1] But over the years a group of unsightly characters began to congregate there. We don't know the attraction of the location for them. Maybe it was because it was near a gate…maybe because it contained a water source…maybe because it boasted a covered shelter area of sorts beside it.[2] Or perhaps…it was the rumor of the angel that visited the waters.[3]

It was said that an angel of the Lord would come down and stir up the waters. The first person to get into the pool after the waters were stirred was cured of disease.[4] Great companies of the blind and lame – even the paralyzed – just lived at the pool. What once had been a spot of beauty and comfort became the town eyesore with all the invalids cluttering the small area.[5]

But they had to stay. No one knew for sure when the waters would be stirred, so they had to be present at all times. The edges of the pool were lined with men and women pushing one another aside, trying to get the best spot. The blind tried to make friends with the sighted so they would know when the waters they couldn't see began to stir. Perhaps they even dangled their feet into the pool, feeling for the slightest movement. After all, what sighted person would give up his own healing just to inform a blind man that it was a good time to jump in?

And what a commotion when the water stirred! The sick and lame jumping…falling…pushing to get in the water. The splashing about…the looking around to see who had been first…then the great escape back to the side of the pool to dry off and wait for the next time.[6]

Off to the side sat a man. He had been an invalid for 38 years[7] – but perhaps he was older than that. He might have been into adulthood before the accident occurred that left him unable to move. Or maybe it was a sickness that came upon him in his childhood – and he never recovered.

Whatever the source, it led him to a lonely world of seclusion from normal life, family, and friends. He was confined to the poolside with those who shared his plight. Maybe he had been enthusiastic at first. Eager to be just feet away from the healing he needed. But all too soon, he learned the chaos of the stirring water. He fought with his limited mobility to make his way into the water, but he needed help. And clearly at this location, no one helped another.[8]

Fear overtook him – how would he get back *out* of the water once he got in? What if no one was willing to step in and assist him? After all, if he drowned, he would be one less person they'd have to fight with next time the waters stirred.

As time passed, so did his hope. There was no point. He wouldn't get well. He would die at the side of the pool just like he'd seen so many others do. Someone would get word to a relative and they'd reluctantly put aside their duties to collect his body.

But this day, a new man wandered about the pool.[9] It was unusual to have visitors; most people avoided the motley crew out of repulsion or fear of contamination. Perhaps this man had a relative here. Maybe he was here to gather a body – had someone died?

The man seemed to be asking questions – maybe he was looking for someone in particular. Well, enough people here knew everyone that his services wouldn't be needed. Never mind that he'd been here almost four decades. Even with seniority, he didn't matter. But the man moved closer to him and soon was directly over him.[10]

The eyes were kind. They seemed unafraid of illness and even a little compassionate. No – *very* compassionate. He asked questions. What happened? How long have you been here? And then, *Do you want to get well?*[11]

What kind of question was that? Was it a challenge? Did this man – this stranger – think he was still sprawled out here after thirty-eight years because he actually *enjoyed* the confinement? Did this man find it a purposeful thing that he'd never been able to get down into the water? *Do you want to get well?* What kind of a question was that?

Trying to keep a respectful, even tone in his voice, the man replied, "Sir, I have no one to help me into the pool when the water is stirred. While I am trying to get in, someone else goes down ahead of me."[12]

There. That should silence him. Perhaps he hadn't thought of that little detail…that he needed help getting into the water. That he *had* tried…time and time again…and it just never worked because he wasn't fast enough. Because someone just a little less impaired beat him to the healing.

The man had perhaps wanted to lash out this answer, but kept it civil in hopes that the man, once aware of the truly dire situation, would stay around for a bit and help him. Maybe the concern was genuine enough to hope for that.

Even as a dozen hypothetical scenarios played in the invalid's mind, he was aware of words coming from the Man's mouth.

"Get up! Pick up your mat and walk."[13]

The man shook his head and sighed heavily. Hadn't this Man heard anything he'd just said? He had been here for thirty eight years! He couldn't walk. He could barely drag his twisted body. What kind of cruel visitor waltzes in, insults his disability, and then challenges him to do the one thing he cannot?

And yet – something already felt different. Maybe he had feeling where once he was numb. Perhaps a heaviness felt lifted or an involuntary twitch struck, notifying him that what once was broken was now whole.[14]

The man began to test his fingers…his toes…his arms and legs…his back and neck…everything worked! He could move! He could bend! He could stand…he could walk![15]

He picked up his mat – which he intended to throw away at the first possible location. He wanted to be rid of its filth and memories. But he picked it up because he *could*! He could carry it and move![16]

When Jesus arrived at the mat of the invalid, He gave him healing. He met the need the man saw as the most critical. But just a while later, He met him again, at the Temple.[17] This time he gave him a true healing that even the man did not fully realize he needed. Jesus said, "See, you are well again. Stop sinning or something worse may happen to you."[18] Yes, the man needed a physical healing. He needed to be freed of life beside the pool. But even more than that, he needed his soul set free. He needed to understand that a body paralyzed is nothing compared to a soul paralyzed. That would keep him from enjoying eternal life – a punishment far worse than any earthly disease.[19]

December 17

He also saw a poor widow put in two very small copper coins.
Luke 21:2

She may have been elderly, barely able to make the walk to the Temple any longer. But she just as easily could have been young – recently widowed and without a brother-in-law to marry in the place of her husband, as law allowed.[1]

So little is said of this woman except she was poor and she gave two very small copper coins to the Temple treasury.[2] We don't even know for sure that she met Jesus face to Face, because Scripture only says He saw her put in the money.[3]

But Jesus didn't usually let someone pass by who was in need of a blessing.

How difficult it must have been for her to go to the Temple that day – and all days she went. Maybe not because it was physically challenging for her to move around, but because every time she went, she encountered the same crowd.

Rich men and women loudly plunked their bags full of coins into the collection plate.[4] They wore their finest and carried lavish bags, bulging on all sides with the coins they'd ferreted from their massive wealth.[5] They may have even prayed a ceremonial blessing, bringing attention to their so-called sacrifice as they deposited it within the Treasury.

Perhaps they stood around to applaud their friends and co-laborers as they too brought an abundant amount of gold and gave it lavishly and loudly to the Lord.

She felt torn.

On one hand, she ached to slither in, unnoticed, make her meager offering, and vanish without anyone being the wiser that she had been there.

Yet how she longed to linger as they did – not to be noticed, but to worship. Jehovah Jireh[6] had cared for her even in her poverty. She did not understand why life came to her as it did. Why her husband had been taken from her when she loved him so and was not ready to be without him.

But even in her grief, she felt the loving arms of God surrounding her as David had written.[7]

Even in her want, she had what she needed.

And for that, she felt compelled to worship. Giving was a part of her worship. She did not have much to give. Were she to disappear, no one would miss her offering, and she knew it.

But she felt an inexplicable connection with God as she made her way into the Temple courts and placed what she had in the Treasury.[8]

She knew man looked at the outward appearance but God looked on the heart[9] and she chose to believe God looked upon her heart each time she appeared in the courts and gave what she had been instructed to give.[10]

That particular day, there seemed to be a great stirring within the Temple. The spectacle at the collection plate seemed even more exaggerated than normal. What was the cause?

Then she saw Him – in the corner. The great Jesus.[11] She had heard about Him. Perhaps she hoped He wouldn't see…wouldn't notice her meager pittance.

But she became aware of His voice – and attention pointed at her. She lowered her head, hoping to evaporate into the crowd of people milling about. But she knew she was still seen by Him – she could feel His eyes watching her move toward the plate.[12]

She listened.

"I tell you the truth – this poor widow has put in more than all the others. All these people gave their gifts out of their wealth; but she out of her poverty put in all she had to live on."[13]

Tears flowed.

Jesus knew. He did truly see her heart, just as the teachers had said. No one else ever saw the point in her offering. No doubt she had seen the scoffs. The eyerolls. The smirks. She had noticed the hands that covered whispering mouths and the fingers pointing behind empty bags recently void of their offerings.

No one else understood it wasn't the amount she gave – it was the spirit in which she gave it. She had nothing to give – but she gave from it anyway. Often it was her last coin. The one she might have used to buy food.

But she knew that to offer it up was to receive it back, good measure pressed down, shaken together, running over.[14] She knew it was God's money before it was ever hers[15] and to recognize that was to acknowledge her complete dependence on Him.

Perhaps she raised those tear-rimmed eyes to meet the Savior's that day in the Temple. The two of them may have shared a heart's exchange as He conveyed to her that she was blessed beyond any of the wealthy that scattered about in showy submission.

As she left the Temple that day, the woman likely did not walk out into a sum of wealth in reward for her spirit. She may not have stumbled upon a husband to support her. No doubt nothing visible changed in her life.

But her spirit was renewed because the Spirit of God had seen it. She had been affirmed by Jesus in a way that no one else ever could affirm her.

His arrival in her small and unseen world, no matter how indirect it had been, proved this truth: the Comforter had come to tell her that the eyes of Heaven had roamed about the earth looking for a heart faithful to the Lord[16] - and she had been seen.

December 18

⸙

But Jesus answered, "No more of this!" And he touched the man's ear and healed him.
Luke 22:51

The night was certainly an eventful one, compared to most – at least for the members of the chief priests, the teachers of the law, and the elders.[1] This night was not spent in the Temple reading and teaching from the scrolls. This night was not spent in the company of friends, enjoying music and fine wine. This night was not spent quietly at home with family.

This was the night the leaders had waited so long to see.[2] For months these men had followed Jesus – not out of reverence or a desire to learn, but rather out of a desire to trap Him.[3] They wanted one mistake from Him. It didn't seem like much to ask. After all, who doesn't make a mistake now and then?

Jesus.

This they learned rather quickly.[4]

Finally they resorted to carefully devised schemes to trap the Great Teacher. They'd followed Him so closely that they became the earliest form of paparazzi. They set up masterfully designed scenarios, certain *this* one would cause Him to stumble and say something...anything...that would give them grounds to prosecute and silence Him once and for all.[5]

Even that was to no avail.

At last, their opportunity presented itself. Or rather himself. Judas Iscariot, one of Jesus' own disciples, approached the leaders and teachers of the law with an offer to betray Jesus right into their hands.[6] Satan had entered his spirit[7] and he agreed to accept money in exchange for the betrayal.[8] He promised to tell them when the moment was right, and they agreed to be ready to move, no matter the day or the hour.[9]

The servant of the high priest was anxious for the appointed time to arrive. What a welcome change of pace this would be from the daily duties of fetching scrolls and standing outside the Holy of Holies listening for the bell tied around the priest's waist to ring as he moved about inside.[10] This day would not be a day of scheduling meetings and carrying trays of wine. This would be a day of action. Of excitement. A day when his master and the entourage of leaders would finally smile instead of furrowing their brows in frustration.

When the moment came, it was night. Judas arrived and informed the High Priest that Jesus would be going to the Mount of Olives.[11] He said to them, "The one I kiss is the man; arrest him and lead him away under guard."[12]

The servant watched anxiously as the High Priest called together all the chief priests, all the teachers, all the elders, all those who had so tirelessly schemed alongside him. He insisted that they approach the Garden armed.[13]

Even the servant carried a sword and a club. Not often did his job call for such an opportunity and he felt excitement surge through his blood. He had a front row perspective for this attack, because his master was the leader of the throng. He walked along beside him, glancing back occasionally to see the crowd of leaders and servants growing thicker and louder.[14]

On the other side of his master, the servant saw Judas' face, jaw tightly set. He walked purposefully, showing no emotion. The servant knew that Judas' relationship to Jesus was similar to his own with the High Priest. He thought of himself…would he be able to betray his own master? He doubted it. But yet, for thirty pieces of silver, perhaps…[15]

His thoughts were brought back to the task at hand when he saw in front of him a small gathering of men. One of them was Jesus. In the dark, it was hard to see which one, though the servant had seen Him many times before in the temple courts.[16]

The angry crowd of teachers and elders stopped, but Judas kept walking forward. He walked straight up to Jesus, called Him "Rabbi," and kissed Him.[17] The servant blinked at the demonstrated respect of Judas' greeting. How could this man call one of his best friends "My Teacher"[18] and greet Him with a respectful kiss and then step back so the mob behind the servant could overtake Him?

While the servant continued to sort out his feelings about the brazen disciple turned betrayer, he caught sight of movement coming his way. One of the men beside Jesus apparently carried a weapon of his own.[19] Before the servant knew what was happening, he saw a sword coming rapidly toward his head. He reacted as quickly as he could, twisting his head aside.

Searing pain blasted down the right side of his head. He felt something warm on his face. Putting his hand up to the side of his head, he found blood spurting from a gaping wound. He looked down and saw his ear lying on the ground.[20]

His ear!

The man had cut of his ear!

The servant barely knew whether to cry out in pain or pass out from the sight of the blood. The High Priest and the crowd behind seemed frozen and silent.

Jesus moved, and no one stopped Him.

But Jesus wasn't running away. As He bent to the ground, His voice spoke sternly, yet lovingly to His disciple. "No more of this. Put your sword back in its place."[21]

The servant watched through a squint of great pain, as Jesus picked up his severed ear and put it back up to the side of his head.[22] He anticipated a rush of pain as the exposed nerves were touched, but in fact, the pain seemed to disappear.

Yes, the pain was gone entirely. And the noises he heard weren't just coming from his left ear. He could hear rustling to the right.

Hesitantly, the servant lifted his hand to touch his head. The gaping hole was gone. Blood no longer flowed. He ran his finger around the side of his ear and didn't even feel so much as a crease. Sound flowed, dare he say better than ever?

The sound that flowed was Jesus' voice: "Am I leading a rebellion, that you have come out with swords and clubs to capture me? Every day I sat in the temple courts teaching, and you did not arrest me. But this has all taken place that the writings of the prophets might be fulfilled."[23]

The servant knew of the writings of the prophets. He had heard them over and over as he served the High Priest. It was real. All those things were real.

The One had arrived. The One who was soon to be oppressed and afflicted…led like a lamb to the slaughter…by oppression and judgment taken away…cut off the from the land of the living…for the transgression of people – stricken, assigned a grave with the wicked, though he had done no violence.[24]

In fact, He had restored what violence had sought to destroy. The servant touched his ear again. He had met Jesus. And though the crowd of elders and leaders pressed around him to take this Jesus into custody,[25] the servant knew that in Jesus' arrival, he met the One who brought life and healing even as others sought to bring Him death.

December 19

Pilate then went back inside the palace, summoned Jesus and asked him, "Are you the king of the Jews?"
John 18:33

It was early morning[1] – the end of a work week. Friday.[2] Pilate, no doubt, like everyone else in the working world, was just ready to put in his required time and enjoy the weekend. Rest. Relax.

Reshape the course of history. That would be exactly what would happen, but as the sun crept up into the sky, Pilate didn't even know it.

He was summoned. Asked to go outside. A criminal awaited. It was so early! Why couldn't they wait a while longer? But the mounting noise of voices told him he should move quickly.[3] Perhaps he could dismiss the case...or at the very least, issue a continuance of some sort.

Pilate looked at the crowd gathered before him with a man in the midst, clearly the accused. "What charges are you bringing against this man?"[4] His voice conveyed his irritation with this early morning nuisance.

The designated speaker of the crowd shouted back, "If he were not a criminal, we would not have handed him over to you."[5]

Pilate had no time for this sort of game-playing. If that's all the clearer they could be about the offense, he was done.

"Take him yourselves and judge him by your own law."[6] He turned away even as he tossed the advice in their direction, but he was stopped by their response.

"But we have no right to execute anyone."[7] So they sought execution. It was going to be a long day. Pilate turned aside and retreated into his palace, to the comfort of his own turf.[8] If only he could have been on vacation now...or even sick in bed. But no. He was present and well and clearly *not* about to escape the demands of the people and this man they brought to him.

Pilate had heard the accusations – *We found this man undermining our law and order, forbidding taxes to be paid to Caesar, setting himself up as Messiah-King.*[9] But he needed to know more than accusations. He needed to know the heart of this Man who called Himself the Messiah-King. So he sent for Him. Not for public questioning, but for a meeting in chambers.[10]

When Jesus arrived, Pilate wasted no time. "Are you the king of the Jews?"[11] Perhaps Pilate cared less about the answer from a matter-of-court perspective and much more from a matter-of-truth perspective. He needed to know. This Man...who had healed the sick[12] and raised the dead[13] and confounded the learned teachers of the law.[14] Was He real?

Pilate craved a straightforward answer, but found the response of a question posed back to him: "Is that your own idea, or did others talk to you about me?"[15]

There was nothing disrespectful in His tone, but the question caught Pilate by surprise. Perhaps he was unwilling to let down the guard around his own questioning heart enough to answer truthfully. Or maybe his law-mind took over and he responded as he had always been taught... question for question.

"Am I a Jew? It was your people and your chief priests who handed you over to me. What is it you have done?"[16] He wanted to know. He felt in his heart this Man had done nothing to deserve this overblown drama, but he desperately hoped He would confess to something punishable.

Jesus was speaking... "My kingdom is not of this world. If it were, my servants would fight to prevent my arrest by the Jews. But now my kingdom is from another place."[17]

Pilate's curiosity was piqued. This Man spoke in riddles. Even though He was under great stress and facing possible consequence of the severest form, His voice remained calm and confident.[18] How could His kingdom not be of this world? Where else would it be? What other place? And yet he couldn't allow himself to be outwitted by the accused. He latched onto the bit of the response he could understand.

"You are a king then!"[19] Perhaps now he could find something about Jesus that would allow him to be clearly declared innocent *or* guilty.

"You are right in saying I am a king. In fact, for this reason I was born, and for this reason I came into the world, to testify to the truth. Everyone on the side of truth listens to me."[20] Jesus sat back, watching to see if those words would resonate in the mind of the governor.[21]

Pilate thought of his own life. Did he know his own reason for living? Certainly he had established a life for himself and a reputation as a respected political figure.[22] But was that all there was to this life? This Man before him seemed so confident of His calling. His purpose. And truth...He came to testify to the truth?[23]

Pilate may not even have realized the words slipped audibly from his lips as he pondered that last part...*What is truth?*[24] If this Man came to bring truth, what crime was that? In fact, if only Pilate could have a few more moments with Him...to find out the truth himself.

As it was, the noise outside told him he had stayed in questioning long enough. He went before the people to find the crowd had grown both in size and volume.[25] He cried out to them, "I find no basis for a charge against him. But it is your custom for me to release to you one prisoner at the time of the Passover. Do you want me to release 'the king of the Jews'?"[26] His heart willed them to accept this Man. For them to realize they'd made something of nothing.[27] Pilate had only just met the Man, but he met Truth personified and he knew the Truth should live on.

But the crowd screamed for the release of Barabbas – a convicted criminal.[28] Pilate's stomach churned. His own wife pled with him to let Jesus go.[29] And amid all the chaos, Jesus stood, silently. Not begging for his life. Not insisting his innocence.[30] The wisdom of Solomon would have pointed to his release based on that alone.[31] Yet the crowd grew intense and angry and Pilate felt pressured into a decision.

His hands shook to match his trembling voice as he spoke his verdict to the crowd: "I am innocent of this man's blood. It is your responsibility!"[32] But even as he washed his hands in the basin provided to him, he could feel the stain seep deeply within his skin.

Truth arrived to Pilate's heart that day. Innocence arrived. Calm arrived. And yet he had given in to fear and thrown the Truth to the people bent on silencing it. Jesus was led from his presence and Pilate never spoke to him again. But the conversation held within the privacy of the chambers surely spoke to him over and over for the rest of his life.

It is as you say...My kingdom is not of this world[33]*...for this reason I was born, and for this I came into the world, to testify to the truth. Everyone on the side of truth listens to me...*

Everyone on the side of truth...

...listens...

...to me...[34]

December 20

A certain man from Cyrene, Simon, the father of Alexander and Rufus, was passing by on his way in from the country, and they forced him to carry the cross.
Mark 15:21

Simon didn't intend to meet anyone that day…at least not anyone in a crucifixion procession.

Why was he even there? He was a long way from home, especially in the days of slow, manual transportation.

We know so little about him…he was old enough to be a father,[1] but were Alexander and Rufus young boys struggling to keep up with his stride, or were they fathers themselves? Was he on his way to visit them and their growing families, or had he come this way in search of something to improve the quality of their tiny lives? Was he in town or business or pleasure? Had he perhaps permanently relocated to Jerusalem from his native land?

To Simon, it felt like a case of being in the wrong place at the wrong time. The crowd was large[2] and curiosity rose in his mind. What could be happening to create this much of a stir?

Then he saw him. A man struggling to hold up the rough and splintery beam of a cross.[3] What had he done? Simon's mind raced with possible scenarios…murder at the top of the list. Whatever he had done must have been horrid for him to be as beaten and bloodied as He was.[4]

Simon asked passers-by for the story and found himself surprised by the response. Blasphemy?[5] Rebellion?[6] Those were the charges leading to *this*?

The soldiers who surrounded the struggling man laughed loudly and poked him with their spears. They kicked at him and he heard some mockery about a kingdom and prophecy. One soldier fed off the scorn of another and they grew louder as they kicked and poked and whipped him.[7]

Simon could hear the wailing of women following the entourage…no doubt the man's family, protesting His unjust sentence.[8]

He have pushed through the crowd in order to get a better glimpse – maybe even to see if he could discern for himself whether or not the man was deserving of this punishment. After all, he seemed barely able to crawl under the weight of the cross. Simon was sure he was weak from blood loss and humiliation.

Before Simon knew what was happening, he found himself recruited by a soldier. Yanked from the crowd. Roughly solicited for the job as cross-bearer.[9]

Perhaps at first he resisted and tried to fade back into the crowd as he had been just seconds earlier. But there was no fighting the adrenaline-filled authority of a Roman soldier. He had no choice but to submit to the task at hand. The rough hands that had grabbed him pushed him viciously toward the bleeding, stumbling man.

Simon sensed that the soldiers who nearly slammed him on top of the convicted did not do so out of any form of compassion. They didn't care about the blood that moistened the dirt underneath his feet or the sweat that drenched his clothing. They weren't moved by his gasps for breath or the groans he long since gave up stifling.

They just seemed impatient to move the parade along. Their solution was to throw another into the mix. Simon had been the *other* they found.

Simon lifted the beam, trying his best to carry the weight for the weakened man on the ground. He heard women behind him calling out the name *Jesus* through their tears – that must be His name.[10]

Jesus…the same Jesus Who had just a week ago been the local hero?[11] That was the Man beneath the blood and dirt? The Jesus Whose fame spread far and wide as the Man who could heal[12] and even bring life from death?[13] What had happened? How was He now on His way to execution for crimes that seemed petty for this treatment?

The cross was surprisingly heavy. Simon knew from the amount of wood that rested across his shoulder, that the cross should weigh no more than fifty pounds. Yet he found himself stumbling…and his soul felt so heavy. This cross wasn't just wood. It was wood infused with the world. Cells of sin sank into his shoulder and rested heavily on Simon's back.[14]

No wonder Jesus struggled to carry His cross. No wonder He agonized. Even free from the weight of the wooden beam, He struggled in anguish. He used His hands to find His way, step by step, prodded forward by the bit of the soldier's whip.[15]

Simon himself felt the sharp bite of the whip a few times as he stepped too close to Jesus. The mocking directed at the Man rolled backward and grasped Simon as well. Shaking fists, loud laughter, clods of dirt, even spit, rained down on both men as they made their way forward.[16]

They had to stop for Simon to shift the load and for Jesus to half-stand and continue on the way. Simon had heard the final destination would be Golgotha,[17] and he knew they weren't far, but the road seemed to stretch on longer than it should. The cross grew heavier and Simon found his breaths growing weaker and shorter. Sweat poured from his own face.

How had Jesus carried the cross as far as He did?

When they reached Golgotha, Simon let the cross fall to the ground, and though the weight of the beam rested in the dirt, the heaviness in his soul seemed fixed.

There was no gratitude from the soldiers – no nod of acknowledgment, even. They were already reaching for a hammer and long, sharp nails.[18]

But even as Simon stepped aside, he found His eyes locked with Jesus'. No words exchanged…but Jesus' dark eyes, brimming with grief and exhaustion, spoke the thanks that His mouth couldn't form. As the soldiers roughly grabbed Him and began to strip his garments from His body,[19] Simon knew in a way that no one else could, just how heavy sin could be.

Inaudible understanding passed between their eyes, and Simon knew.

He had arrived at the feet of the Savior of the world.

He had felt the sin of the world on his back.

His own sin mingled with the sin of others.

And this Man felt it a thousand times more heavily.

That sin would kill the Man.[20] And from that silent conversation that passed between them, Simon knew Jesus was willing to carry that weight.[21]

When Jesus arrived in Simon's path, He shared with him the weight of sin. And Simon watched as that sin was cast away forever and new life was born from the weight of a cross.[22]

December 21

When they came to the place called the Skull, there they crucified him, along with the criminals – one on his right, the other on his left.
Luke 23:33

The man was guilty.[1] Perhaps the robbery had been his first,[2] but it was a big job he tried to pull, and he was caught in the act. Maybe he hadn't even really wanted to be a part, but he was drawn in by those he should have known better than to befriend. And then again, maybe this was the last in a long string of robberies. This time his luck ran out. Dozens and dozens of jobs went unsolved by the authorities, and then this one went bad.

No matter the situation, the man was guilty and he knew it. Though he dreaded the torment of death by crucifixion, he knew he deserved the punishment.[3]

Criminals were crucified all the time. Perhaps he'd even watched a few executions in his day. Maybe some of them had been men he'd worked alongside in robbery jobs – but they were found out and he had gone free. He knew it would be a painful way to die, but then again, he knew the risks when he committed the crime.

That day he would hang on a cross alongside two others on their crosses.[4] Another convicted robber would die.[5] Maybe the other criminal had been a part of the same robbery ring…caught during the same crime.

But the third Man…something was different about Him. He had arrived with quite an entourage,[6] and He was badly beaten.[7] So much so, in fact, the man noticed someone else carried His cross for Him.[8]

But there was no fear in His eyes. No anger about Him. The thief sensed exhaustion and the deepest sort of grief he'd ever seen a man express. But where most criminals carried an air of resignation as they approached their execution site, this Man carried a sense of purpose and determination.

As though even in death, He had a task to accomplish.[9]

Three crosses elevated to the sky. The Man hung in the middle of the two robbers.[10] The criminals seemed almost invisible to the crowd that pressed against the middle cross. Soldiers were gambling for the Man's clothing.[11] Women wept violently just a few yards away.[12] On the outskirts of the crowd were very somber onlookers...who really didn't look up much at all.[13] And pressing in at the foot of the cross was a crowd of loud mockers who pushed every energy into torturing the Man.[14]

The robber heard the name Jesus.

He had heard of Jesus.[15]

And then he heard Jesus – gasping through pain, "Father, forgive them, for they do not know what they are doing."[16]

This Man...He was forgiving those who killed him. And even as He did so, the crowd continued to jeer. "He saved others; let him save himself if he is the Christ of God, the Chosen One."[17] They taunted Him and challenged Him over and over to climb down off the cross and prove He really was the Son of God.[18]

Then the man heard a new voice. It came from the other side of the execution line. The other robber, even while fighting his own death, joined in with the crowd below. "Aren't you the Christ? Save yourself and us!"[19]

The man thought for a moment about how wonderful it would be to see the Son of God rip His arms and legs free from the nails that pinned Him to the cross.[20] To see Him climb down and walk into the very crowd that sneered at Him. To silence their filthy mouths. And then to see Jesus turn and call him down from his own cross. He could have another chance at life. A chance to be the man he knew he should have been before he got mixed up in a life of crime.

But before he allowed his wistful daydream to continue, he called over to the man on the other side of Jesus: "Don't you fear God, since you are under the same sentence? We are punished justly, for we are getting what our deeds deserve. But this man has done nothing wrong."[21]

Jesus turned to look at the man and there was a glimmer of love in those pain-filled eyes. Perhaps even some relief mixed in as Jesus knew the man understood He was the Son of God and He was innocent of sin.

As the two stared at one another, even in the very hour of death, the robber blurted out, "Jesus, remember me when you come into your kingdom." [22]

Why had he said that? He was a guilty criminal, rightfully convicted of not only a crime – but of sin. Deep, dark sin that so blackened his heart, he wasn't even sure he felt the full depth of the sin anymore.

Why would Jesus want to remember him? The man was fairly certain it was for deeds such as this that Jesus hung beside him in the first place.

But Jesus was speaking.

"I tell you the truth, today you will be with me in paradise."[23]

The words were spoken between gasps for breath. Pain wracked Jesus' body, but even in that moment, He extended grace and forgiveness to one whose sin bore down upon Him right then.

The robber knew Jesus wasn't going to amaze the crowd by climbing down from His cross that day. The robber knew both of them had seen their last sunrise – and before the next sunset, life would be gone from their bodies.

But their spirits would live on.

That day...they would be in paradise.

For the thief, Jesus' arrival meant the offering of eternal life that very day. Because Jesus *didn't* climb down from the cross, the thief could die knowing that eternal life in Heaven had just been handed to him. Jesus' outstretched arm extended to him a way of life everlasting.[24]

Even as Jesus died, He gave life to the repentant soul. And Golgotha[25] became a picture of history that day. Jesus' Spirit stood between one who would accept Him and one who would reject Him.

But to him that would receive Him, He gave the power to be called the son of God.[26]

December 22

And when the centurion, who stood there in front of Jesus, heard his cry and saw how he died, he said, "Surely this man was the Son of God."
Mark 15:39

The Bible doesn't say how old the centurion was, but for him to have advanced in the military ranks far enough to have command of one hundred soldiers indicates this was not his first week on the job, nor his first crucifixion.

There were undoubtedly certain perks that came with being the charge soldier in the Roman empire. He could pick and choose which tasks he wanted to personally oversee and which ones he wanted to delegate to the lesser members of his force. If he saw fit, he could assign himself to the more public moments of grandeur and leave the grunt work to the new guys.

After all, he had served his time as a new guy. He had done the daily law enforcement patrols. He had made arrests and carried out the sometimes ridiculous orders of the high commanders. His hard work and unquestioning attitude had paid off and now he had his own group of men. He took seriously his job of raising them – almost as if they were sons. He wanted to be known as the centurion with the best force beneath him.

The trial and sentencing of Jesus had been a big deal. No doubt the centurion had heard rumblings of the uprising in the days and weeks before it even took place.[1] He knew it would be a high profile case,[2] whenever it surfaced, and he made mental plans to somehow be in the middle of the action.

Perhaps he had lowered himself for just a moment, to be in the parade route from Jerusalem to Golgotha.[3] The escorting of a prisoner was something that no longer held much excitement for him, usually. He would have delegated such a task without hesitation…but this was Jesus.

So he put aside his normal protocol and joined the procession. He even let his men carry on more raucously than usual. They were having great fun proclaiming this man was the King of the Jews. He laughed at their impromptu crown of thorns and scepter of reeds that they pushed upon the accused.[4]

He cast his own whip a few times and roughly insisted that the procession move along. Maybe he was even the one who solicited Simon of Cyrene from the crowd of onlookers and ordered him to carry the cross when Jesus fell to the ground.[5]

The scene at the execution site was loud. Executions seemed to be a thing of sport for the general population. They were usually well attended, but this one was even more populated.[6] The soldiers settled in for a long day, for such a type of death normally took hours, sometimes even days.

As the centurion looked on and kept an eye out for general order in the crowd, his men gambled for the clothing they had ripped from Jesus' body.[7]

He allowed the men to participate in the mockery, which only incited the crowd to jeer more loudly.[8]

Jesus' pain seemed excruciating – which was not uncommon for someone dying by crucifixion, yet there was something out of the ordinary about this man. The pain wasn't just a physical pain, but his very soul seemed to agonize.[9]

Of course there was wine being passed among the soldiers, and given that this was an execution, there was also some myrrh at hand, usually intended as a burial spice. The centurion ordered that the two be mixed and offered to Jesus to help deaden some of the pain He seemed to carry.[10]

Jesus refused the drink.[11]

Something in the centurion's heart began to soften and wonder. Why would this man, obviously in such great pain, refuse a tonic to sooth his anguish?

The centurion hushed his own insults and began to observe the man on the cross.

He eavesdropped as Jesus offered eternal life to the guilty criminal beside him.[12] He watched as the thief's face relaxed in peace and he accepted his fate even more than before.

The sky grew darker and a storm appeared to brew in the distance. This was the part of executions the centurion hated most. They must go on, regardless of the weather. Though it was the middle of the day, darkness hovered over that hillside with no apparent intention of leaving.[13]

Suddenly, the centurion heard Jesus cry out loudly, "My God, My God, why have you forsaken me?"[14]

The very words shook the centurion's soul and genuine fear gripped him. If Jesus was forsaken by God, then there would be no hope for anyone else! Oh if only he could have had a conversation with Him like the thief did…

Another loud cry escaped from Jesus' lips, and His body sagged on the cross. He didn't move again. No other breath escaped His lips.[15]

The centurion's observations were interrupted by a great earthquake that shook the ground.[16] As he steadied himself at the foot of the cross, he knew.

He knew the cross that supported him in that moment held the Son of God.[17]

He thought back to the moment when Jesus had called to His Father. He had seen the abrupt death that engulfed Him. That sort of thing just didn't happen in crucifixions. He had seen enough to know.

The centurion spoke aloud – to no one in particular. "Surely this man was the Son of God."[18] And right there at the foot of Jesus' cross, he began uttering words of praise that seemed to not stop coming from his lips.[19]

That day, Jesus arrived in the life of the man who declared His death. That day, the centurion arrived in the presence of the Son of God. That day he learned that the grace and glory of God can saturate even death itself.

December 23

Taking Jesus' body, the two of them wrapped it, with the spices, in strips of linen. This was in accordance with Jewish burial customs. At the place where Jesus was crucified, there was a garden, and in the garden, a new tomb, in which no one had ever been laid.
John 19:40-41

Joseph of Arimathea. A Sanhedrin. A member of the Jewish council described as a good and upright man.[1]

And a coward.

A coward because he only consented to be a secret disciple of the Lord.[2] He was afraid of what would become of his job[3] if the men who sought to destroy the kind and gentle King[4] knew he believed every word the Man said. He was afraid of their taunting, their anger, and their gossip.

He drank in every word Jesus said and yet he was neither hot nor cold. Only lukewarm.[5] A fair-weather friend. A heart that longed to be devoted, yet a spirit afraid to be counted faithful.

Alongside him was Nicodemus,[6] a Pharisee and member of the Jewish ruling council.[7] He sneaked in to see Jesus under the shadows of evening, desperate to find the truth about this Man.[8] It was to Nicodemus that Jesus introduced God's great love for the world that caused Him to send His one and only Son, that whoever believes in Him shall not perish but have eternal life.[9] It was to Nicodemus that Jesus divulged no one could enter the kingdom of God unless he was born of water and the Spirit.[10]

Two men.

Two cowards.

Two searching hearts.

Brought to the foot of the cross holding one Savior of the world.[11]

Did they arrive before Jesus' pain-wracked body drew its final breath and He cried out in a loud voice, *Father, into your hands I commit my spirit…*[12] *It is finished…?*[13]

Or did they simply arrive as the shadow of evening approached and the blood began to dry on His lifeless frame?[14]

Had they hurried in hopes of admitting aloud in His final moments that He was right and they were sorry to have been so afraid…but found they were too late?

Why is it that death propels action more than life?

Joseph, the one who had so carefully guarded his secret following of the Savior, boldly entered the presence of Pilate and asked permission to take the body of Jesus.[15] Perhaps his chin quivered ever so slightly as he informed the equally emotion-stricken governor of Jesus' time of death.[16] Both men knew the unspoken Truth.

Pilate granted permission,[17] and Joseph returned to join Nicodemus at the foot of the cross.[18] Carefully, they lowered the lifeless body of their Lord from His cross of execution.[19]

The face that had so earnestly and lovingly spoken to them words of gentle truth and conviction now relaxed in death. The gentleness they knew, the forgiving and hopeful Spirit, lay crumpled in their arms.

Joseph and Nicodemus stared into the face of One who had embraced their searching hearts and beckoned them to follow.

And for the first time, the two men publicly associated themselves with the Savior.

No more secrets.

No more hiding.

They didn't care who stood two hundred yards or two feet away. They didn't care what happened to their jobs or their reputations.

From the storehouses of their wealth, they pulled out enough burial spices to bury a king. They lavished myrrh and aloes upon the King of kings.[20]

With every bit of the gentleness and mercy He displayed in preparing their souls for a place in the Kingdom,[21] they prepared His body for a place in the tomb.[22]

With every bit of the patience and love He had bestowed upon them in the secret moments when they questioned Him about eternal life,[23] they wrapped His body for what they thought would be His eternal life.[24]

With every bit of the generosity He had showered on them as He laid the foundation of truth in their hearts, they carefully laid his body in a tomb of their own provision.

With every bit of the protection He had shown to them by respecting their position in the Council, they rolled a stone against the entrance to the tomb to protect His body from thieves and animals that would seek to destroy it.[25]

And with that, the men left.[26]

We don't know what happened to them after that day. Did they give up their posts on the Council to instead carry out the traditional mission of public disciples?

Did they remain employed as before but simply cease hiding their devotion to the Savior?

We don't know.

And though we know the day of Jesus' crucifixion was not the day Jesus first arrived in their lives, it was the day they first arrived in His.

Two men.

No longer cowards.

Transformed into public disciples of Christ.

December 24

Jesus said to her, "Mary."
John 20:16a

Mary stood alone outside an empty tomb. She didn't conceal her tears, nor could she have done so if she'd wanted.[1]

Confusion overwhelmed her mind. She thought back to a day that seemed so long ago, but really was not so many years earlier. A young man arrived…a Man named Jesus, and He had given her a new start. She was possessed by not just one…but seven demons.[2] Her life was no longer her own and she was despised by society. And yet Jesus had seen her and been so moved with compassion that He delivered her of the stronghold over her life.

Out of love and gratitude she had followed Him. She and other women whose lives had been touched by the Gentle Savior gave up everything they had and were in order to support the ministry of Jesus.[3] She had supported Him even in death…following closely behind His cross all the way to Golgotha.[4]

The tears started Friday morning when Pilate sentenced Jesus to death.[5]

The tears intensified Friday afternoon as He breathed His last.[6]

The tears hadn't stopped all weekend while she waited for the Sabbath to end so she could hurry to the tomb and tend to His body. He deserved a proper burial and she intended to see to it personally that He received it.[7]

But when she arrived at the tomb, His body was gone.[8] Anger had risen in her heart – even in death they couldn't leave Him alone? These leaders and teachers hadn't tortured Him enough in life? They had to steal Him in death? Anguish dug even more deeply into her soul as the thoughts swept through her mind once more.

Some of the disciples had been there with her just moments before,[9] but they had gone back home.[10] She didn't know why they left her, but she couldn't bring herself to leave the opening of the tomb that should have held Jesus' body.

She bent over to look in one more time – wondering if perhaps her eyes had been so blinded by tears that she just didn't see the Body.[11] Maybe if she looked again, it would be there right where it should be.

Much to her surprise, the tomb was not empty – but it wasn't because the Body had suddenly appeared. Angels – clothed in white – stood in the tomb.[12] She had heard talk of angels, but she'd never seen them. And yet now they stood before her and even spoke to her.

"Woman, why are you crying?"[13]

Mary felt a little strange talking to angels, but she was desperate for answers. "They have taken my Lord away, and I don't know where they have put him."[14]

The hurt and grief rose up so greatly in her heart that she had to turn away. As she turned from the tomb, a man stood before her.[15]

It wasn't the disciples, returning to be with her. She didn't know this man. Perhaps he was the gardener. It would make sense. He would want to be out tending to his property after the Sabbath.[16]

He spoke to her, "Woman, why are you crying? Who is it you are looking for?"[17]

Hadn't he heard her answer to the angels in the tomb? They had just asked her that very question!

Perhaps she quickly hoped he *hadn't* heard her conversation with the angels. After all, maybe she was the only one who could see the angels, and if someone found her conversing with herself, he might think the demons had returned to possess her. And if they did return, she would be stuck with them for life. Jesus wasn't here to cast them out again.

Mary rushed into an explanation before the gardener could think too much of the situation. She pled with him, "Sir, if you have carried him away, tell me where you have put him, and I will get him."[18] She could understand this man might not want Jesus of Nazareth resting in his tomb for all eternity. Given the way He had died, His presence in that tomb might be inviting trouble for the good gardener. She wouldn't blame him for wanting the Body gone. But Mary just needed to get to that Body and demonstrate her love by giving it a proper preparation. She realized she had said she would get the Body if he'd just tell her where he had put it. She wasn't sure how she planned to transport it, but it didn't matter. She had to find it.

And then The Voice broke into her thoughts.

Mary.[19]

Warm relief encased her heart. It was His Voice. She could hear it. Her memory hadn't lost the sound of His gentle Voice.

But wait.

It *was* His voice. Not just memory speaking to her soul.

She turned to face the Man. "Rabboni!"[20] Her teacher had come back. He was here. He wasn't in the tomb because He wasn't dead! He was alive! He was touching her hands! He was gripping her arms as her knees buckled beneath her. She grasped tightly to His clothing and held onto Him in a grip that continued alongside her tears.

Jesus pushed back and looked into her eyes. That gentle Voice spoke again, "Do not hold on to me, for I have not yet returned to the Father. Go instead to my brothers and tell them, 'I am returning to my Father and your Father, to my God and your God.'"[21]

Mary nodded vehemently, understanding His call to her life. Though she ached to stay in the Garden with Him, to feel the comfort of His presence and hear the gentleness in His Voice, this wasn't the plan.

Suddenly, words He had spoken before made sense. He would have to die, but He would overcome death, He would rise again in three days[22] and He would go back to the Father.[23] The next part of the plan had yet to take place.

And she, Mary Magdalene, the once-demon-possessed, had been called by God Himself to begin the story of the Gospel. Jesus had arrived once, but this day He arrived again. And this time, He commissioned her life and soul. He had saved them once from the stronghold of demons. He had saved them again three days before when He conquered the power of death. And now He called her to go and tell the news of what she had seen and heard.

The Risen Savior arrived to Mary's heart in a meeting as sacred as His arrival to another Mary's heart over thirty years before. But this time He didn't arrive in need of tender care. He came to offer a bold affirmation to go forth and share the news of His love.

December 25

For God did not send his Son into the world to condemn the world, but to save the world through him.
John 3:17

God saw.

God Himself, seated on a Heavenly throne, high and exalted, honored by the seraphs and angels,[1] saw.

He saw people, created in His own image,[2] who were desperately in need. The sight was not a new one for Almighty God. Hundreds of years earlier, He had gazed into the Garden of Eden, a perfect paradise He had made for the man Adam,[3] and He saw a need. He saw a man in need of companionship, and He arrived to form a woman to complement, help, and sustain him.[4]

And in every human life that followed the creation of Adam and Eve, God saw need. Never did a need go unmet. The love of the Creator for the creation of His hand caused Him to send rain on the righteous and the unrighteous alike.[5]

As the years went by and the Hand of Heaven provided for the people of earth, God saw the greatest need of all: a Savior. He vowed through the prophet Isaiah that the people walking in darkness would see a great light.[6] A child would be born. A son would be given.[7] But not just any son. *His* own Son. His *only* Son.[8]

Sitting upon the Throne of Heaven, God saw needs that could only be met by meeting the Savior Himself…

…a formerly demon-possessed woman…in need of assurance that the One who saved her once could save her still.

…two cowardly religious leaders…in need of the courage to publicly admit their association with the King of kings.

…a centurion leading his troops in punishing the derelicts…in need of the understanding that the grace and glory of God is more powerful than the crucifixion of the convicted.

…a thief caught up in the habit of sin…in need of forgiveness for his heart more than in need of punishment for his crime.

…a man from Cyrene on a journey…in need of strength to help bear the weight of the sin of the world.

…a governor…in need of prioritizing the difference between the truth of the law and the Truth of the Spirit.

…a servant dutifully assisting his legalistic high priest…in need of physical healing and a High Priest more interested in the spirit of the law than the letter of the law.

…a widow giving what she couldn't afford to give…in need of heart affirmation that her sacrifice was accepted by Heaven.

…a lame man…in need of Miraculous Power to rescue him from wasting away while waiting on mystical powers to heal him.

…a man afflicted with dropsy…in need of someone to overlook the protocol of the day of rest and offer him rest from his suffering.

…a rich young ruler…in need of someone to explain what mattered most in life and to love him even as he walked away.

…a short and greedy tax collector…in need of someone to see him amid the crowd and to show him the power of giving rather than taking away.

…a Samaritan woman…in need of someone to see her mind and heart, not just her body and to offer her something of value and not just a proposition.

…little children…in need of a blessing from someone who understood what it was like to be an inquisitive, energetic child.

…a bleeding woman…in need of someone to look past the cleanliness rules and simply touch her to restore what illness had demanded of her.

…a demon possessed man…in need of someone to dare to venture near him and allow him a life beyond the graveyard.

…a sinful woman…in need of someone to understand that the desire of her heart went beyond prostitution to deep adoration.

…a mourning mother…in need of someone to see that the body on the coffin was her last hope and bring life from death.

…an outspoken fisherman…in need of a career change even though he didn't see in himself the potential to be any more than he was.

…an elderly man patiently awaiting a promise…in need of eternal rest, but unable to receive it until the Consolation of Israel arrived.

…three Magi anxiously searching the skies…in need of a star that would point them to a new king, not realizing they would find *the* King.

…a group of bumbling shepherds…in need of a change of pace from their daily duties of sheep-watching.

…a righteous young man…in need of a life much more extraordinary than he ever would have imagined possible for himself.

…a young woman who found favor in the eyes of the Lord…in need of a Savior just like all the rest.

Just like all of us.

In His great love, God gave up the One He loved most. His one and only Son. He prepared Jesus for a mission of love and compassion…a mission that would culminate in the ultimate love gift. A life sacrifice that made it possible for us to be called the children of God.[9] He sent Jesus to meet the hurting and to change their lives in gentle tenderness.

And as you celebrate the remembrance of His birth in Bethlehem, you cannot offer back to Him a greater gift than the offering of your own life as a sacrifice. Not in crucifixion, but as a holy and pleasing sacrifice of worship.[10]

This same Savior who arrived to love and touch and bless…wants to be the Savior to you.

The day of His birth probably wasn't December 25th. Giant flakes of snow didn't fall from the sky and carolers didn't lurk outside the stable door singing songs of good cheer. No hot chocolate with marshmallows and decorated sugar cookies awaited Mary, Joseph, the shepherds, or anyone else. No festively adorned fir tree stood in the corner of the stable, and no brightly-colored gift wrap hid any well-kept secret.

The first Christmas was so very different from the celebrations of this year. But it was no less cause for celebration. Whether it was day or night, hot or cold, a Gift of God came from Heaven's Halls to bring new life… not just to the arms that welcomed Him, but to hearts that would welcome Him for all time forward.

And though none of us were there that first night…and none of us were there for the thirty-some years that followed…we're not so different from those who met the Savior. And His presence, though not in tangible flesh, is very real…and still His greatest gift.

Endnotes

December 1

1. Luke 1:35
2. Psalm 139:16
3. Luke 2:7
4. John 19:25
5. Luke 2:7
6. Luke 1:28, 30-33, 35, 37
7. Luke 1:46-55
8. Luke 1:34
9. Luke 1:38
10. Luke 1:46-49
11. Luke 2:19, The Message

December 2

1. Luke 2:7
2. Matthew 1:16, 18
3. Matthew 1:19
4. Matthew 1:20-21
5. Matthew 1:24
6. Matthew 1:25, The Message
7. Matthew 1:22-23
8. Matthew 1:19
9. Matthew 1:21
10. Matthew 13:55
11. Matthew 2:13-16
12. Luke 2:43-46
13. Luke 2:49
14. John 19:25-27
15. Matthew 1:20-21
16. Matthew 13:55-56
17. Colossians 1:15

December 3

1. John 1:29
2. Luke 2:9
3. Luke 2:10-12
4. Luke 2:13-14
5. Luke 2:15

6. Luke 19:10, Matthew 25:40
7. Revelation 21:27
8. Luke 2:16
9. Luke 2:12
10. Luke 2:16
11. 1 Peter 2:24
12. Luke 2:10
13. Luke 2:20

December 4
1. Matthew 2:1-2
2. Matthew 2:2
3. Matthew 2:2
4. Conclusion drawn from the distance they traveled and the amount of gifts they brought – in a day when modes of transportation were primitive and gifts such as the ones they brought very costly.
5. Matthew 2:7
6. Matthew 2:3, 2:13
7. Matthew 2:8
8. Timeline conclusion drawn by Herod's decree to kill all boys two and under – Matthew 2:16
9. Matthew 2:10
10. Matthew 2:10, The Message
11. Matthew 2:11
12. Matthew 2:11
13. Matthew 2:11
14. Matthew 2:11
15. Matthew 2:11
16. Luke 2:19
17. Matthew 2:11, The Message
18. Matthew 2:11
19. Matthew 2:12

December 5
1. Simeon's age is speculated based on his proclamation in Luke 2:29 that he can die in peace – and because his story appears alongside the story of Anna the prophetess, who, in Luke 2:36 is said to be "very old."

2. Many traditional readings of Jesus' birth are pulled from Luke 2, but stop at the end of verse 20, when the shepherds leave the manger. Simeon's story begins in verse 25.
3. Luke 2:25
4. Luke 2:26
5. Luke 2:26
6. Methuselah was the oldest living man ever recorded in history. According to Genesis 5:27, he lived for 969 years.
7. Luke 2:27
8. Luke 2:22-24
9. Luke 2:28
10. Exodus 13:1-2 records God's command for every firstborn male to be consecrated to Him. Leviticus 12:1-8 explains the timeline for a mother had to go to the temple for purification from childbirth. Leviticus 12:4 says she had to wait 33 days to be purified from her bleeding, which would make Jesus a little over a month old at the time of this event.
11. Luke 2:29
12. Luke 2:52

December 6
1. Luke 2:46-47, 52 and Luke 4:14-15
2. Matthew 4:25
3. Luke 5:1
4. Luke 5:5
5. Luke 5:1
6. Luke 5:2-3
7. Matthew 16:17-19. Simon Peter's name given to him by his family was Simon. Jesus gave him the name Peter. He is referred to by both names throughout Scripture.
8. Luke 5:1, 5
9. Luke 5:3
10. Luke 5:6
11. Luke 5:3
12. Luke 5:4
13. Luke 5:4 , The Message
14. Luke 5:5
15. 1 Samuel 16:7
16. Luke 5:6

17. Luke 5:6
18. Luke 5:7, 10 and Matthew 4:21
19. Luke 5:7
20. Luke 5:8
21. Luke 5:10
22. Luke 5:11
23. Luke 5:11
24. Matthew 4:22

December 7
1. Luke 7:14
2. Luke 7:12
3. Luke 7:12 declares this boy was an only child and the woman was a widow. The implication is given that he was her only hope, which also implies that the woman no longer had parents to care for her according to Jewish law. (Leviticus 22:13, Deuteronomy 25:5)
4. Deuteronomy 25:5 indicates that a son would typically assume the role of providing for his mother if she were widowed.
5. Luke 7:12
6. Exodus 22:22, Deuteronomy 14:29, Deuteronomy 24:19-21
7. Luke 7:14
8. The deceased's age is not specified, but Jesus calls him "young man."
9. Luke 7:13
10. Lazarus' tomb, described in John 11:38, was called "a cave with a stone laid across the entrance." Jesus' tomb, described in Matthew 27:60 was called a "new tomb that he had cut out of the rock. He rolled a big stone in front of the entrance to the tomb..."
11. Luke 7:13
12. Luke 3:23 states that Jesus was "about thirty years old when he began his ministry." Most theologians conclude that his ministry lasted approximately three or four years because of the number of Passover celebrations John indicates Jesus attended: (John 2:13, 5:1, 6:4, 11:55)
13. The Bible does not specifically say that Jesus' mother walked in the procession with the other women from the cross to the tomb (Luke 23:55), but John 19:26-27 indicates she was at

His crucifixion and that Jesus' best friend, John, reached out to her with compassion at Jesus' bidding.

14. Luke 7:14
15. Luke 7:14
16. Luke 7:15
17. Luke 7:15
18. Luke 7:14-15
19. Luke 7:15
20. Luke 7:16
21. 2 Samuel 3:31, Esther 4:3, Ezekiel 27:31, and Amos 8:10 indicate that this was traditional activity for mourners.

December 8

1. Matthew 23:1-39 contains Jesus' assessment of the Pharisees' ostentatious behavior.
2. Luke 7:36. According to Matthew 26:6 and Mark 14:3, the Pharisee's name was Simon the Leper. In Luke 7:40, Jesus does address him as Simon.
3. Luke 7:49 mentions the presence of other guests. Although the account in John 12 may refer to a separate incident, it does mention that Judas was present. Jesus generally traveled with the disciples, so it is assumed that they were present at this meal.
4. Luke 7:37
5. Although an account of Jesus' feet being anointed by a woman is mentioned in each of the four gospels, Luke is the only one who specifically says she was a sinful woman. It is possible that his account refers to an anointing separate from the ones listed in Matthew, Mark, and John, which seem to indicate the woman was Mary of Bethany, who was never said to be a prostitute. I am writing according to the account given in Luke – where the woman is said to have lived a sinful life – and I am assuming prostitution was her sin.
6. Luke 6:37-38
7. Luke 7:37
8. Matthew 23:13 says that the Pharisees "shut the kingdom of heaven in men's faces. You yourselves do not enter, nor will you let those enter who are trying to." The woman would have fallen into this category.

9. Luke 6:38
10. Though it may refer to a separate incident, Mark 14:5 says that the perfume used in the anointing could have been sold for "more than a year's wages."
11. Luke 7:37
12. Luke 7:36 says Jesus reclined at the table.
13. Luke 7:38
14. Luke 7:39
15. Luke 6:38
16. Luke 7:38
17. 1 Corinthians 11:5-6
18. Luke 7:47
19. Luke 6:38
20. Luke 7:38
21. Luke 7:39
22. Luke 7:44-47
23. Luke 6:38
24. Luke 7:50

December 9
1. Luke 8:30
2. Luke 8:27
3. Luke 8:27
4. Luke 8:27
5. Luke 8:28-29
6. Luke 8:28
7. Luke 8:28
8. Luke 8:29-30
9. Luke 8:27, 29
10. Luke 8:31
11. Revelation 9:1, 2, 11
12. Luke 8:32
13. Luke 8:32 simply says Jesus "gave them permission" to enter the herd of pigs.
14. Luke 8:32-33
15. Luke 8:35 does not say Jesus provided the clothing for the man, but it does say when others arrived on the scene, they found the man "dressed and in his right mind."
16. Luke 8:34-35

17. Luke 8:34-35
18. Luke 8:37
19. Luke 8:37
20. Luke 8:38
21. Luke 8:39
22. Luke 8:39
23. Luke 8:39

December 10
1. Luke 8:43 Tradition has indicated that this was some sort of disorder related to her reproductive organs, but the Bible does not specifically state this.
2. Leviticus 15:25-30
3. Leviticus 15:19, 26-27
4. The Bible does not specifically say that those unclean from bleeding had to practice this, but Leviticus 13:45-46 indicates that a person unclean because of an infectious skin disease had to announce his or her presence and live in isolation as long as he or she was unclean. It is possible that the same was required of someone chronically ill from a bleeding disorder.
5. John 2:1-11
6. Matthew 8:1-4
7. Luke 8:26-39
8. In that day, women were not considered equal to men and for reasons of propriety, could not always freely approach a man to speak with him.
9. Leviticus 15:25-30
10. Luke 8:44
11. Luke 8:43
12. Luke 8:41-42
13. Luke 8:44
14. Luke 8:44
15. Luke 8:45
16. Luke 8:47
17. Luke 8:48
18. Luke 8:49

December 11
1. Mark 10:13 says the children were "little."
2. Scripture doesn't say if this incident immediately followed the one listed before it, but if it did, Mark 10:1 says "crowds of people came to him, and as was his custom, he taught them."
3. Mark 10:6-9
4. Isaiah 53:2
5. Mark 10:13
6. Mark 10:13
7. Mark 10:14
8. Mark 10:15
9. Mark 10:16
10. Acts 9 tells the account of Saul (also called Paul – see Acts 13:9) and his conversion from a life of sin to a life of ministry.
11. Acts 4:36 introduces Barnabas. Acts 9:27 begins to describe his ministry in the early Church.
12. Acts 16:1 begins the account of Timothy's involvement in the Church.
13. Acts 1:15, 2:42, 2:44, 4:32
14. Acts 2:22-47
15. Mark 10:14
16. Romans 12:1
17. Hebrews 12:2

December 12
1. John 4:6
2. Tradition indicates the woman went to the well at a time of day when most others did not, because she tried to avoid their remarks of disdain over her life's choices.
3. Assumption made based on John 4:18 when Jesus referenced how many times she had been married and that her current companion was not legally her husband.
4. John 4:9
5. John 4:7
6. John 4:9
7. John 4:10
8. John 4:18
9. John 4:11

10. John 4:12
11. John 4:13-14
12. John 4:15
13. John 4:16
14. Numbers 27:1-11 indicates that legal matters such as property and inheritance, were handled only among men. This particular passage tells of a time when women appealed for the rights to such matters in the event that there was no male heir.
15. John 4:17
16. John 4:17-18
17. John 4:19
18. John 4:21-24
19. John 4:25
20. John 4:26
21. John 4:28-29

December 13
1. Luke 19:1 indicates that Zacchaeus lived in Jericho.
2. Luke 19:2, 8
3. Luke 19:2
4. Luke 19:7 gives the people's opinion of Zacchaeus.
5. Luke 19:8
6. Luke 19:1
7. Luke 19:3
8. Luke 19:3
9. Luke 19:3
10. Luke 19:3
11. Luke 19:4
12. Luke 19:4
13. Luke 19:3
14. Luke 19:5
15. Luke 19:6
16. Luke 19:7
17. Luke 19:6
18. Luke 19:8
19. Luke 19:9

December 14
1. Matthew 19:22
2. Luke 18:18
3. Mark 10:17
4. Matthew 7:7
5. Mark 10:18
6. Matthew 10:19
7. Matthew 23:13-36 gives Jesus' account of how the Pharisees (who would have influenced the teachings this young man had received) were really good at knowing and enforcing legalistic parts of Jewish law, but in the process, they were missing the point. Mathew 5:17-20 says that Jesus' intention was not to do away with the law as they knew it, but to focus on the *intent* behind the rules. He said that unless people's righteousness could surpass what was being taught, they wouldn't enter Heaven.
8. Mark 10:20
9. Mark 10:21
10. Luke 19:10
11. Mark 10:21
12. Mark 10:22
13. Mark 10:22
14. Luke 16:13
15. Ephesians 2:8-9 says that we are saved by grace through our faith in God, and that this salvation is a gift from God… nothing we can earn through accomplishments or possessions. That way everyone has an equal chance.
16. Luke 10:27 shows the depth of devotion God desires from His children.
17. Mark 10:23

December 15
1. Even though we observe Sunday as a day of rest and worship, in that day Saturday, the seventh day of the week, was the day of rest. This followed the words of the fourth commandment in Exodus 20:9-10.
2. Exodus 20:9-10

3. Matthew 12:1-2, Luke 13:10-16, John 5:9-10, John 5:16-18, and John 9:13-17 show examples of the Pharisees' careful attention to following the rules of the Sabbath.
4. The Bible does not specifically state the traditional Sabbath day practices, but Matthew 23:5-7 tells of the Pharisees' love of finery and attention.
5. Exodus 20:9-10 stated that no work was to be done on the Sabbath...by anyone, including servants. Even during the years of wandering in the wilderness, God made a provision for the Sabbath day's food to be gathered and prepared the day before. – Exodus 16:22-26
6. Luke 14:1
7. Luke 14:1
8. Matthew 9:11 and Luke 7:39 show examples of the Pharisees' thoughts of Jesus' choice to mingle with "sinners."
9. Luke 21:1 shows the practice of making monetary offerings at the Temple. Luke 16:14 says the Pharisees loved money.
10. Matthew 22:15 – the Pharisees were looking for a way to trap Jesus in His own words and actions.
11. Matthew 25:40
12. Luke 14:1
13. Luke 14:2
14. Luke 14:2
15. Luke 14:2-4
16. Luke 14:3
17. Luke 14:4
18. Luke 14:4
19. Luke 14:4
20. Luke 14:5-14
21. Luke 14:4

December 16
1. John 5:2. The description of the pool leads us to believe it would have been a beautiful place at one time.
2. John 5:2
3. John 5:4 – This verse is not listed in the main text of the NIV, but it is footnoted saying that early manuscripts included these words: "From time to time an angel of the Lord would come down and stir up the waters. The first one into the

pool after each such disturbance would be cured of whatever disease he had."
4. John 5:4
5. John 5:3
6. John 5:7
7. John 5:5
8. John 5:7
9. John 5:1, 6
10. John 5:6
11. John 5:6
12. John 5:7
13. John 5:8
14. John 5:9
15. John 5:9
16. John 5:9
17. John 5:14
18. John 5:14
19. Ezekiel 18:30

December 17
1. Deuteronomy 25:5-6 allowed a provision for the brother of a dead man to claim the deceased's wife and provide an heir for him.
2. Luke 21:1-2
3. Luke 21:2
4. Matthew 6:2
5. Luke 21:4
6. Jehovah Jireh is the Hebrew name for God that demonstrates his provision, as declared in Genesis 22:13-14.
7. Psalm 32:10
8. Luke 21:2
9. 1 Samuel 16:7
10. Deuteronomy 14:22 and Proverbs 3:9 show the admonition of the Lord for everyone to honor Him with the first tenth of all their income.
11. Luke 21:1
12. Luke 21:2
13. Luke 21:3-4
14. Luke 6:38

15. Job 41:11
16. 2 Chronicles 16:9

December 18
1. Luke 22:52
2. Luke 19:47
3. Matthew 22:15
4. Luke 20:26
5. Matthew 22:34-35, Luke 22:2, John 11:51-53
6. Luke 22:4
7. Luke 22:3
8. Luke 22:5
9. Luke 22:6
10. Exodus 28:34-35 states that bells were to be worn on the hem of the priestly garment so they could be heard when he was inside the Holy of Holies, a place only the High Priest could enter.
11. Luke 22:39, John 18:2
12. Matthew 26:48
13. Matthew 26:47
14. John 18:3
15. Matthew 26:15-16
16. Mark 14:49
17. Matthew 26:49
18. *Rabbi* means "My Teacher"
19. Luke 22:49
20. Luke 22:50
21. Luke 22:51, Matthew 26:52
22. Luke 22:51
23. Matthew 26:55-56
24. Isaiah 53:7-9
25. Matthew 26:57

December 19
1. John 18:28
2. John 19:14 says it was the Day of Preparation, which was Friday...the day the people prepared for the Sabbath, which actually began at sundown Friday night and lasted until sundown Saturday night.

3. John 18:29
4. John 18:29
5. John 18:30
6. John 18:31
7. John 18:31
8. John 18:33
9. Luke 23:1, *The Message*
10. John 18:33
11. John 18:33
12. Luke 8:47
13. Luke 7:14-15
14. Luke 2:46-47
15. John 18:34
16. John 18:35
17. John 18:36
18. Matthew 27:14
19. John 18:37
20. John 18:37
21. John 18:28
22. John 18:28
23. John 18:37
24. John 18:38
25. John 18:38
26. John 18:38-39
27. Matthew 27:18
28. John 18:40
29. Matthew 27:19
30. Matthew 27:14
31. 1 Kings 3:16-27 tells of Solomon's judgment between two women who insisted their own child was alive and the other's child was dead. When Solomon declared the one living child should be cut in two and half given to each woman, the true mother insisted the child be given, whole, to the other woman. He knew by that offering that she was the real mother.
32. Matthew 27:24
33. John 18:36
34. John 18:37

December 20
1. Mark 15:21
2. Luke 23:27
3. Mark 15:21
4. John 19:1-3
5. Matthew 26:65
6. Luke 23:14
7. Matthew 27:27-31
8. Luke 23:27
9. Mark 15:21
10. Luke 23:27
11. Matthew 21:1-11 is the account of Jesus' Triumphal Entry into Jerusalem just one week earlier. That day, people paid honor to Him.
12. Luke 8:46
13. Luke 7:14-15
14. 1 John 2:2
15. Mark 15:19
16. Mark 15:17-20
17. Mark 15:22
18. John 20:25 records the disciple Thomas' declaration that he would not believe Jesus had risen from the dead until he could touch the crucifixion nail scars in Jesus' hands.
19. Matthew 27:35
20. Mark 15:37
21. Mark 14:35-36
22. Matthew 27:51-53

December 21
1. Luke 23:32
2. Matthew 27:44
3. Luke 23:41
4. Matthew 27:44
5. Matthew 27:44
6. Luke 23:27
7. Luke 22:63
8. Luke 23:26
9. Isaiah 53:4-10
10. Luke 23:33

11. Matthew 27:35
12. Luke 23:27
13. Luke 23:48-49
14. Luke 23:35
15. John 19:19
16. Luke 23:34
17. Luke 23:35
18. Matthew 27:40, Luke 23:37
19. Luke 23:39
20. John 20:25 indicates that Jesus was nailed to the cross.
21. Luke 23:40-41
22. Luke 23:42
23. Luke 34:43
24. John 3:16
25. Matthew 27:33
26. John 1:12

December 22
1. Matthew 26:3-4
2. Matthew 14:13 – Jesus typically had large crowds surrounding Him, leading others to assume that whenever Jesus was involved, whatever happened would be a significant event.
3. Mark 15:1 – Jesus' trial began at Pilate's quarters in Jerusalem and his execution site was Golgotha, as listed in Mark 15:22
4. Mark 15:16-20
5. Mark 15:21
6. Luke 23:27
7. Mark 15:24
8. Luke 23:35
9. Mark 15:34
10. Mark 15:23
11. Mark 15:23
12. Luke 23:43
13. Mark 15:33
14. Mark 15:34
15. Mark 15:37
16. Matthew 27:51-53
17. Mark 15:39

18. Mark 15:39
19. Luke 23:47

December 23
1. Luke 23:50
2. John 19:38
3. John 19:38
4. Matthew 26:3-4
5. Revelation 3:15-16
6. John 19:39
7. John 3:1
8. John 3:2
9. John 3:16
10. John 3:5
11. Mark 15:46
12. Luke 23:46
13. John 19:30
14. Mark 15:42
15. Mark 15:43
16. Mark 15:44-45
17. John 19:38
18. John 19:39
19. Mark 15:46
20. John 19:39-40
21. John chapter 3
22. John 19:40
23. John chapter 3
24. John 19:40
25. John 19:41, Matthew 27:60
26. Matthew 27:60

December 24
1. John 20:11
2. Mark 16:9
3. Luke 8:1-3
4. Mark 15:40-41
5. John 19:6
6. Luke 23:46
7. Luke 23:55-56

8. John 20:1-2
9. John 20:3-4
10. John 20:10
11. John 20:11
12. John 20:12
13. John 20:13
14. John 20:13
15. John 20:14
16. John 20:15
17. John 20:15
18. John 20:15
19. John 20:16
20. John 20:16
21. John 20:17
22. Luke 9:21-22
23. John 7:33

December 25
1. Isaiah 6:1-4
2. Genesis 1:27
3. Genesis 2:8
4. Genesis 2:18
5. Matthew 5:45
6. Isaiah 9:2
7. Isaiah 9:6
8. John 3:16
9. 1 John 3:1
10. Romans 12:1

CPSIA information can be obtained at www.ICGtesting.com
Printed in the USA
BVOW011345211112

306146BV00003B/297/P